GW00367013

PAPER · 276

Asia's International Role in the Post-Cold War Era

PART II

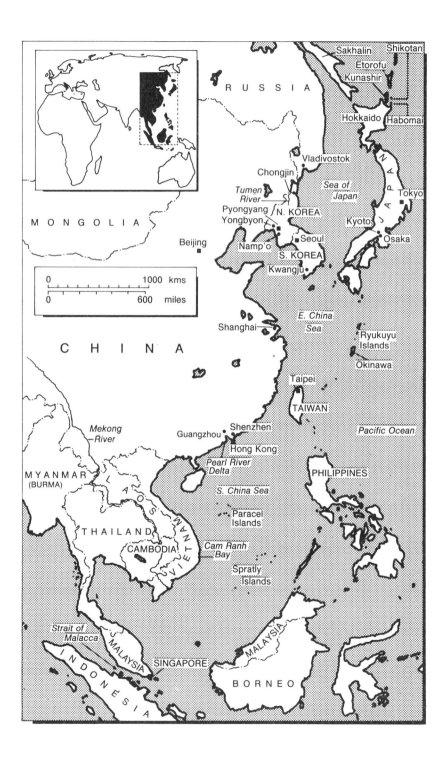

CONTENTS

Glossary

ALCM	Air-Launched Cruise Missile
ANIE	Asian Newly Industrialized Economy
APEC	Asia–Pacific Economic Cooperative
ASEAN	Association of South-East Asian Nations
ATBM	Anti-Tactical Ballistic Missile
AWAC	Airborne Warning and Control System
CBM	Confidence-Building Measure
CFE	Conventional Armed Forces in Europe
C^3I	Command, Control, Communications and Intelligence
COCOM	Coordinating Committee for Multilateral Export Controls
CSCA	Conference on Security and Cooperation in Asia
CSCE	Conference on Security and Cooperation in Europe
CTB	Comprehensive Test Ban
EAEC	East Asia Economic Caucus
EFTA	European Free Trade Association
ERDA	Energy Research and Development Agency
FPDA	Five Power Defence Arrangement
GATT	General Agreement on Tariffs and Trade
GPALS	Global Protection Against Limited Strikes
IAEA	International Atomic Energy Agency
ICBM	Intercontinental Ballistic Missile
INF	Intermediate-range Nuclear Forces
INFCE	International Nuclear-Fuel Cycle Evaluation
ISRO	Indian Space Research Organization
juche	self-reliance (North Korea)
MLRS	Multiple-Launch Rocket System
MTCR	Missile Technology Control Regime
NACC	North Atlantic Cooperation Council
NAM	Non-Aligned Movement
NIC	Newly Industrializing Country
NPT	Nuclear Non-Proliferation Treaty
OAPEC	Organisation of Arab Petroleum-Exporting Countries
ODA	Official Development Assistance
OECD	Organisation for Economic Cooperation and Development
PKO	Peacekeeping Operation
PMC	Post-Ministerial Conference
Pu	plutonium
SAARC	South Asian Association for Regional Cooperation
SDF	Self-Defence Force
SDI	Strategic Defense Initiative
SEATO	South-East Asia Treaty Organization
SLBM	Submarine-Launched Ballistic Missile
SSM	Surface-to-Surface Missile
START	Strategic Arms Reduction Talks
Te	tellurium
UNDP	United Nations Development Programme
UNTAC	United Nations Transitional Authority in Cambodia
WEU	Western European Union
WTO	Warsaw Treaty Organisation

What Security Regime in North-East Asia?

DR CHUNG-MIN LEE

Along similar lines as the continuing security debate in Europe, the parallel discourse in Asia has emphasized the need for innovation, structural modification and new thinking. It has also been suggested that, because of the uncertainties associated with a post-bipolar world, Asia needs to stress the notion of a 'common Asian home', buttressed by an indigenous security mechanism.

This may be achievable over the longer term, but in the medium term powerful national sentiments and forces, which are unlikely to be significantly modified, will probably prevail. This is not to imply that the spectre of war looms over the horizon, nor that potentially significant tensions will not be diffused, only that the search for a common security framework in North-east Asia, however well intentioned or designed, faces a number of challenges, at least for the duration of this decade.[1]

What, then, are the alternatives to such a framework in the interim? This question will be addressed using four main propositions: that national strategies, as distinct from collective strategies, will be on the rise in North-east Asia as a whole in the post-Cold War era; that processes of reconciliation or normalization may loosen, but not fundamentally alter, the geopolitical equation; that the evolution of domestic political forces and regime change in the case of selected actors are likely to emerge as significant determinants of regional security; and that, although key bilateral security relationships will continue to be stressed, their overall utility may well be weakened considerably by post-Cold War national strategies.

The limitations of common security

The end of the Cold War has heralded numerous confidence-building measure (CBM) proposals for North-east Asia. These have ranged from adapting elements of the Conference on Security and Cooperation in Europe (CSCE) process to Asia, proposing 'defensive defence' doctrines and intraregional arms control, and enhancing political/military transparencies.[2] Cumulatively, however, emulating Europe has

The views and opinions expressed in this paper are the author's own and should not be construed as representing the views and opinions of the Sejong Institute.

resulted in a holistic discourse in Asia and, for all its attractions, this has substantial limitations.

Following Europe's example entails a number of assumptions: first, that the end of the Cold War has had a substantial impact on North-east Asia; second, that existing security mechanisms (primarily, but not exclusively, bilateral) can be supplemented (if not supplanted over the long term) by multilateral engagement to promote regional 'cohesiveness'; third, that the rise of new threats – for example, nuclear and non-nuclear proliferation – calls for collective actions and responses; and fourth, that the marginalization of military power and the rise of economic influences dictates new approaches to security issues.

WHAT NORTH-EAST ASIAN COMMUNITY?

If each of these four assumptions are to prove valid in the longer term, a number of countervailing propositions need to be examined in the short to mid-term. To begin with, although the end of the Cold War has had a global impact, the net effect on North-east Asia has not been far reaching.[3] Indeed, it can be argued that national strategies, particularly in the area of defence, will be more relevant in the region precisely because of the end of the superpower contest there. There are significant obstacles to applying regional security maxims in North-east Asia, given the lack of a common security denominator, divergent perceptions of threat (both latent and real) and deeply ingrained historical legacies.

Throughout the twentieth century, all of the major countries in North-east Asia – China, Japan, Russia, North and South Korea – and the United States, have, at one time or another, been at war with each other. How these individual actors will perceive each other's motives in the post-Cold War years remains to be seen, but perceptions are likely to be influenced substantially by contending and contrasting historical experiences.

Any wide-ranging collusion of security interests among these countries is likely to be offset, at least in the short to mid-term, by key internal political transitions, notably in North Korea and China. This factor is crucial, because a common security perspective – and a working multilateral institution – hinges substantially on domestic politics.

How North Korea or China react to the regionalization of security will depend critically on their respective internal political machinations, the *Weltanschauung* of their leaders (present and future) and potentially volatile domestic change, especially in North Korea in the post-Kim Il-sung era. Similarly, it is hard to imagine that Seoul's perception of Tokyo's increasingly robust role in security affairs will not be affected by domestic forces. In more ways than one, domestic politics and regime change are the missing links in forging a common security platform.

From the perspective of alliance management, consideration of an intraregional security mechanism, as distinct from a regional forum, will be constrained by a web of weakened, but still resilient, bilateral arrangements. However, while Beijing has made substantial adjustments to its Korean policy, including establishing official ties with Seoul in August 1992, it has been careful not to undermine its relations with Pyongyang.

In the non-political arena, widely incongruent levels of economic growth, distinct national economic strategies and increasing intraregional competition limit the prospects for economic harmonization. While bodies such as the Asia–Pacific Economic Cooperative (APEC) are now in existence, this 12-member organization is still only in its infancy and is assuredly not an Asian version of the European Community (EC). Nor is it equipped to deal with security issues.[4] Further, bilateral trade frictions – foremost among them those between the US and Japan, but also the increasing US–Sino trade deficit and the Korean–Japanese equivalent – compounded by continuing technology transfer, market liberalization and General Agreement on Tariffs and Trade (GATT) negotiation disputes, suggest that economic harmony, at least in the foreseeable future, is only in the eyes of the beholder.

Moreover, notwithstanding Francis Fukuyama's now famous dictum on the 'end of history', the contest between democracy and communism has not ended in Asia. Indeed there is only a thin veneer of shared democratic values in the region. With the exception of the established democracies (Japan, Australia, New Zealand), all of the other nominal (Malaysia, Singapore, South Korea, the Philippines) and in-between (Thailand, Indonesia) democracies are in different stages of political development. And Asian responses to significant political repression, such as the Tiananmen Square massacre and the events in East Timor and Myanmar (Burma) – not to mention abuses by the Thai military – have been muted.

In summary, the 'Asianizing' of North-east Asian security – by constructing a more durable CBM structure along the lines of the CSCE, adopting non-offensive defence postures, breaking away from established norms and practices, and inculcating democratic values – warrants serious consideration. Yet, as Laurence Martin has noted, the problem is not 'in the realm of machinery, but of style, outlook and sense of identity'.[5] Certainly, the progress which has been made thus far should not be underestimated. The new turn in Washington–Moscow relations, China's commitment to economic reform (despite a political freeze), the engagement of the two Koreas in a series of dialogues and, above all, a measurable decline in the threat of war in the region are all positive outcomes of global détente.

The rise of national strategies
The end of the Cold War in North-east Asia hinges on three principal developments: transformations within the arc of Asian socialism, in-

cluding North Korea, China and Mongolia in the north, Vietnam, Laos, Cambodia and Myanmar in the south; policy responses and adjustments by the United States, Japan and South Korea as well as by Association of South-East Asian Nations (ASEAN) members; and changes in the political roadmap as a result of such developments as Korean (or even Chinese) unification. In addition, how Russia elects to deal with such issues as the preponderance of nuclear forces in the Far East, the unresolved Northern Territories dispute and future relations with North Korea will also have an impact on determining regional stability.

Over time the remaining vestiges of the Cold War in North-east Asia will disappear, but will it usher in a period of 'long peace'?[6] If peace is defined narrowly as the absence of a major war, the answer is most definitely in the affirmative. But intraregional tensions may increase irrespective of developments resulting from the end of the Cold War in the North-east. Indeed, the calculus of regional security will be complicated by three principal forces: nationalism; new power dynamics; and as yet undefined great-power aspirations.

If the Korean peninsula emerges as a unified state by the end of the century, the threat perceptions of the regional powers are bound to be affected. By virtue of its strategic location at the crossroads of Japanese, Russian, Chinese and even American interests, Korea has been subjected to invasions, suzerainty, colonization and occupation. How a unified Korea, but more importantly a unified *and* a relatively powerful Korea, chooses to integrate into the region is still a matter of speculation. But it will certainly be perceived as an actor in its own right, and no longer as a mere extension of great-power rivalry.

China's future role in North-east Asia is another major issue. To remedy the ostracism which confronted it after the Tiananmen Square episode, Beijing has adroitly shored up its security through a series of diplomatic manoeuvres.[7] Yet the degree to which China can accrue significant returns from damage-limitation diplomacy also depends on how it alleviates pressures on the home front, such as the demand for more political freedom as a consequence of rising living standards. And, over the longer term, China's handling of the unification question, not to mention the minorities question (including the future status of Tibet), may surface as potentially divisive issues.

In addition to the roles of China and Korea, which will be examined at greater length below, the evolution of US, Japanese and Russian policies in North-east Asia is also critical. Of these three powers, the United States and Japan are likely to play the most important roles in the region.

For all the talk of imperial overstretch and the continuing decline of US capabilities,[8] the United States' influence in North-east Asia is still quite substantial. No other major power has the political capital, the diplomatic leverage or the key military arrangements to oversee the current process of change within the region. As for Japan, adopting a suitable political role in the post-Cold War era has surfaced as a major national and international issue. Despite reservations at home and abroad, Prime Minister Kiichi Miyazawa's government passed the so-called Peace Keeping Operation (PKO) Bill in the Japanese Diet on 15 June 1992, enabling the self-defense forces (SDFs) to participate in offshore peacekeeping operations for the first time since the introduction of the Peace Constitution in 1947.[9] Japan no longer perceives itself as an 'economic giant' with only limited political influence, and the debate within Japan over its political role has accelerated after its much criticized part in the Gulf War.[10] How Japan opts to articulate its regional security role will have an impact not only on the evolution of the Washington–Tokyo relationship, but also on the future prospects for Korean–Japanese and Sino-Japanese ties.

REDEFINING 'PAX AMERICANA'
The changing balance of power in North-east Asia – caused by the collapse of the Soviet Union, an economically and militarily self-confident China, a more self-assured Japan and the potential emergence of a unified Korea – indicates that the assumptions which have determined the US role in the region can only change.

While the continuing debate within the United States on its post-Cold War global security role shows no sign of an early conclusion,[11] Washington is unlikely in the near future to forgo the security blocs it has developed. But alliance-management needs in the Asia–Pacific region – foremost among them the US–Japan and the US–Korea relationships – will be intensified by the scheduled drawdown of US forces from the region, increasing cost-sharing pressures and the politicization of security.

The April 1990 US Department of Defense report, widely referred to as the 'East Asia Strategy Initiative', or 'EASI', the 'Defense Planning Guideline for Fiscal Years 1994–1999', as well as a series of other official and private studies, all attest to Washington's search for an appropriate security role in the post-bipolar era.[12] Nevertheless, the continuing reconfiguration of US forces in the Asia–Pacific region is likely to be expedited to place the emphasis on streamlining US forces in the region.

Is a US military presence in North-east Asia warranted in the foreseeable future? The short answer is yes, but only if the overall mission can be more clearly defined, and rendered more operationally sustainable and politically acceptable on both sides of the Pacific. While no two Asian countries perceive the US military role in exactly the same way, the US presence has by and large been seen as the most viable security 'equalizer' in the region. (After the deactivation of the US bases in the Philippines, Singapore partially picked up the slack by agreeing to service US warships in the Pacific, an agreement reached during President Bush's visit on 3–5 January 1992.)[13]

Nevertheless, as post-war US engagement in the Asia–Pacific region was forged under Cold War conditions, the overall containment rationale has now been weakened substantially, except in the Korean peninsula. But the US presence will also inevitably change with any wide-ranging *rapprochement* between the two Koreas, or, as is more likely, unification followed by significant political change, particularly in the North. In either case, however, the status of the US forces in the peninsula can no longer be perceived in an essentially linear way. Given such a scenario, on what basis will the United States construct its post-Cold War Asian security policy?

Former Australian Prime Minister Bob Hawke has stated that the primary US security mission in a post-Cold War Asia is to discourage regional powers from acquiring military capabilities which might prove destabilizing.[14] But on what grounds the United States should foot the lion's share of the security burden in order to discourage, if not to deter and even perhaps contain, rivalries between erstwhile allies will be increasingly argued, particularly in the US Senate. As the *New York Times* noted in a recent editorial:

> Even before the Cold War ended, the mission of US forces shifted from containing Communism to keeping potential Asian rivals at arm's length from each other. There's no good reason for America to bear this regional security burden alone as Asian societies grow increasingly rich and powerful . . . A smaller US military garrison [in Korea and Japan] makes good sense, provided Washington also works to build up a new system of regional collective security. *Such a system would provide the best insurance against conflicts between Asian states as Japan raises its military profile in the region.*[15]

In essence, although the argument that US forces are needed in Asia to offset a potential intraregional arms race is good domestic politics for Asia (since it can circumvent the need to justify the continued deployment of US forces in-country), it is inherently poor politics for Washington. Ironically, the basic quandary which confronts the United States stems largely from the success of its post-war security policy in Asia, with the notable exception of Vietnam.

In the 1970s and 1980s, successive US administrations, under rising pressure from Congress, repeatedly asked Japan to increase its share of the common defence burden, for example by furthering its cost-sharing contributions and pumping more resources into the SDF. In the context of containing the Soviet military presence in the Far East, Japan's more robust defence policy was welcomed and actively encouraged.

With the unexpectedly rapid decline of the Soviet military threat in North-east Asia, however, Washington confronts three major tasks. First, it must forge a politically tenable post-Soviet security policy in the region, coupled with a reassessment of China's strategic 'utility'. Second, if the US–Japan relationship is indeed 'second to none' (as stated by the former US Ambassador to Tokyo, Mike Mansfield), Washington should address directly the issue of Japan's role in regional security. And third, the overall drawdown momentum in the Korean peninsula should be implemented, albeit with caution.

THE DECLINING UTILITY OF THE CHINA CARD

Throughout the 1970s and into the 1980s, China's 'strategic utility' in containing the Soviet Union was a primary factor in improving US–Sino relations. It was also argued that China's leverage could be used to diffuse regional problems such as the North–South Korean stalemate and the deepening Cambodian quagmire. However, while the Soviet Union did not ignore the China factor, it responded to the US–China (and peripherally Japan) collusion by increasing its forces in Europe as well as in the Far East. Indeed, the Soviet Pacific Fleet registered its biggest growth just when Washington was emphasizing China's ability to contain the Soviet threat.

Proponents of the engagement school might argue that even if China did not have the ability actively to contain Soviet military forays in the Far East, having a China which was not hostile to US interests was as important as using China in constraining the Soviet Union. As one former US official has noted, 'to be of value to the United States in deterring the Soviet Union, China did not have to do very much; it just had to be there'.[16]

But in the post-Soviet era, continuing to accommodate China in the broader US security framework will become much more difficult, particularly since frictions are already apparent in the US–Sino relationship, but especially since China is likely to go its own way, irrespective of the preferential treatment it has received from Washington. Nevertheless, the temptation to maintain the status quo remains strong, as illustrated by a recent Pacific Forum/CSIS report:

> No one in Asia wants to see a rupture in US–PRC ties. US engagement with this huge country and dialogue with its leaders can be a key determinant in China's future orientation. Without denigrating either American values or policy principles, the US should continue to try to draw China into the world. *The US should also resume contacts at all levels with the Chinese military*, although caution in technology transfer and equipment sales remains warranted.[17]

Others have argued that because China is a great power, 'the United States must limit the hostility in its relationship with China much as it did in superpower relations in the darkest days of the Cold War'.[18] While stable relations with China should be maintained, it does not necessarily follow that China's strategic interests in the region will continue to coincide with Western or, more specifically, with US interests in the post-Cold War era.

Even after the collapse of the Soviet Union, for example, Beijing has continued to increase its defence spending. In a budget submitted to the People's Congress on 21 March 1992, military spending was set at $6.76 billion, an increase of 12% over the level in 1991.[19] As the *New York Times* has reported, China is seeking to project power beyond its shores by 'acquiring air-refuelling capability for its fighter aircraft, by building up a blue-water navy, and eventually by building an aircraft carrier'.[20] China may also hope to retain significant influence in the South China Sea where parts of the Spratly and Paracel Islands have shown evidence of oil, natural gas and phosphorous deposits. This would have the added bonus of sending a clear warning signal to Taiwan. Ironically, Russia is emerging as a potentially significant supplier of a range of weapons systems to China.[21]

In the final analysis, if China chooses to undertake a comprehensive and sustained military drive, it will do so of its own accord prompted by factors ranging from a perceived longer-term threat from Japan, a need to maintain a strategic buffer around the Korean peninsula (particularly after unification) or even as insurance against Russia's future adventurism, with only limited reference to the US.

JAPAN'S SEARCH FOR STRATEGY

If China's quest for potential great-power status is a cause for concern, so too is Japan's search for an appropriate security role in the post-Cold War world. Specifically, how Japan chooses to fulfil the following three objectives will have major implications for regional stability: maintaining deterrence within North-east Asia; responding to regional conflicts and possible violations of peace and security in the international community; and participating in confidence-building measure talks, including arms control negotiations.[22]

Efforts to reassess Japan's security posture obviously did not begin with the global end of the Cold War. As early as 1980, Japan outlined the basic objectives of a so-called comprehensive security policy which stressed the need for self-defence, a multifaceted response to varied national security threats and intermediate efforts to construct a favourable regional security environment.[23] Japan's major concern was that, commensurate with its increasingly robust international economic presence, it could no longer afford to sustain an essentially passive foreign policy, especially when the key pillar of its post-war security mechanism, the US–Japan alliance, was undergoing substantive change.

Cautiously, but with increasing conviction, Japan's policy elite articulated the need for greater involvement in international security matters, particularly since Japan was already making substantial contributions in the form of official development assistance (ODA), UN peacekeeping operations and humanitarian assistance.[24] In essence, if Japan was asked to assume a larger share of the common economic burden, why could it not also do so in the political arena?

As noted above, the post-Cold War security debate in Japan increased markedly in the aftermath of the Gulf War for two main reasons. First, despite the fact that Japan made substantial financial contributions to the multinational effort in the Gulf War (totalling $13bn, the third largest contributor after the United States and Saudi Arabia), it was criticized, essentially, for its 'cheque-book diplomacy'; and second, given such criticism, Japan needed to define more clearly its non-economic contribution to international security.

From Japan's perspective, it was being criticized precisely for taking a position which had long been advocated by the West, particularly the United States: that of increasing its financial contributions to global and regional security. In brief, the feeling within Japan can perhaps best be summarized as follows: Japan's future role in regional security should be debated openly, but it is incongruous to criticize Japan for having followed a policy prescription long advocated by the United States. As one Japanese foreign ministry official noted:

> The changing balance of economic power between the United States and Japan over the past 45 years and the end of East–West confrontation have left Japan no choice but to reassess and redefine its own role in maintaining world peace and stability. This is a matter Japan can no longer avoid considering . . . *Japan must make its own decisions dictated only by its long-term national interests. Japan should not give the impression that it decides only under strong US pressure.*[25]

What role Japan will ultimately undertake in the years ahead is still a matter of speculation. But there are two basic US misperceptions of the Japan question. First, the prevailing view that the US–Japan alliance is the linchpin of US policy in Asia consistently underestimates the importance of continuing change within Japan. For instance, many have argued within the United States that because the US–Japan relationship is so important, technical adjustments will suffice to sustain this relationship in the post-Cold War era. As Alan Romberg and Marshall Bouton have argued, both Japan and the United States have to 'reconceptualize the alliance on a more equal basis, educate their publics about the need to maintain and strengthen it, and rid the dialogue of its adversarial tone'.[26] However, there is a risk that by the time the United States 'reconceptualizes' its relationship with Japan on a more 'equal basis', such a need may well have been overtaken by events.

Second, if the US military presence in the region declines in the 1990s, particularly after Korean reunification, it remains to be seen whether the United States will continue to 'call the shots' on key security issues in the region, including the question of Japan's longer-term regional defence role.[27] Clearly, even if such a situation transpires, it does not necessarily follow that Japan would automatically fill the void left by an American withdrawal.

Instead, as Gerald Hensley, former Defence Minister of New Zealand, has pointed out, the more valid argument is 'not that Japan will remilitarize in the absence of an American presence, but simply that if America pulls back, the Japanese will slowly move to fill the gap'.[28] Also, as many Japanese have noted, if Japan should begin to fill the gap left by a graduated US drawdown from the region it would immediately cause other Asian powers to focus their own national defence efforts on counterbalancing Japan's military growth. However, the fact remains that Japan has been pursuing a sustained defence modernization programme, particularly on its air and sea-lane defence capabilities. As *Jane's Defence Weekly* has noted, 'even without the possibility of an aircraft carrier project this decade, the JMSDF is developing into one of the world's top six navies'.[29]

In the political domain, the debate is ongoing given the wide public support within Japan for assuming a low-key security posture, although a number of Japanese officials have stressed that Japan's assumption of a more direct international security role is necessary. For example, former Japanese Ambassador to Malaysia, Okazaki Hisahiko, outlined the major implications for Japan in the post-Cold War era as follows: the US–Japan security partnership must be maintained, although 'relying exclusively on US support is an irresponsible act'; Japan's defences should be increased since there is no change in the 200-year-old threat from Russia; US interests on the Korean peninsula are declining significantly with the end of the Cold War, although Korea's importance will increase for Japan in the years to come; and Japan's basic security policy is unlikely to change on account of its participation in UN peacekeeping operations.[30]

In the final analysis, Japan is likely to assume a more direct role in regional security issues. As Prime Minister Miyazawa noted in an address to the National Press Club in Washington on 2 July 1992, 'I will assure you that Japan, on its part, *will fulfil its roles and responsibilities commensurate with its national strength and international standing*'.[31] By extension, therefore, Japan already assumes that it can play an active role in securing regional stability based on its increasing national influence and stature in the international community. Just how Japan will manage to fulfil its 'new' responsibility without a significant backlash from the region (already alarmed by the power of the 'Yen Bloc') is not only a central question to be answered by Tokyo's political leadership, but also a test of how it will choose to emerge from its imposed political isolation.

THE KOREA FACTOR

For the first time since the nineteenth century, the Korean peninsula is poised to emerge as a unified and independent regional actor – with substantial implications for the region. Exactly when and how the peninsula will be reunified remains to be seen, but the 'correlation of forces' is likely to be more rapid than is currently assumed. In part, this forecast is based on developments such as the unification of Germany in 1990 and the collapse of the Soviet Union in 1991, but the key factor lies in future developments in North Korea.

Indeed, despite Pyongyang's best efforts to preserve regime stability through a combination of adroit damage-limitation diplomacy, harsh political control and limited economic reforms, the post-Kim Il-sung era will most likely signal the end of the very political system the 'Great Leader' has nurtured since the mid-1940s.

Assessing prospects for North Korea after the death of Kim Il-sung is admittedly situation-specific and speculative. But the entire unification debate and the North–South relationship will move into an entirely different sphere after his death, much as Soviet politics did after the rise of Mikhail Gorbachev, although the net impact will be substantially greater in the North than in the South.[32]

The basic strategy which Seoul has pursued thus far hinges on the following key assumptions: irrespective of such major roadblocks as North Korea's potential nuclear weapons programme, North–South relations *can* be improved, even substantially, through a series of efforts to engage Pyongyang; through such efforts as joint North–South entry into the United Nations and North Korea's acceptance of International Atomic Energy Agency (IAEA) inspections, Pyongyang's policy *vis-à-vis* Seoul is changing, albeit incrementally; and South Korea can afford to take a longer-term view given that, to all intents and purposes, the North–South systemic competition has been decided in favour of the South. But the overall policy of engagement is limited on three main accounts.

First, North Korea's basic strategy towards the South has not changed in substance, although there is an urgency to equate tactical shifts on the part of Pyongyang with real overtures towards Seoul. Second, while agreements have been made, Pyongyang's strategy of accepting broad political principles without specific operational agreements significantly curtails the prospects for unification through negotiation. And third, regardless of intermittent or even substantial progress in inter-Korean relations, the very fabric of North–South relations will be changed irrevocably by developments in Pyongyang in the post-Kim Il-sung era.

In addition, contrary to South Korea's original intention of pressuring Pyongyang through new inroads *vis-à-vis* Moscow and even Beijing, the North has actually responded by increasing its forces to a total of some 1.2m active troops and accelerating its arms production, including the long-range (1,000 kms) *Scud* D mobile SSM (known as *Rodong* 1).[33] Why has Pyongyang reacted in such a manner? Simply stated, it has run out of viable options.

North Korea's basic dilemma is that without endangering the very survival of the regime – together with the all-important support of the nomenclature – it simply cannot afford to undertake the reforms which, however, it must implement in order to assuage popular discontent with a rapidly failing economy. In the interim, and in the absence of a better alternative, North Korea has therefore opted to avoid harsh choices and has focused on retaining whatever economic support it can garner from Japan in the form of compensation if and when formal ties are established.

It has been argued that even if North Korea is confronting a series of difficulties on the home front, Kim Jong-il may well overcome these challenges given his *de facto* control over the party, the armed forces and the intelligence agencies. But even if he currently manages the day-to-day affairs of the North, it does not necessarily follow that his ability to secure power will succeed for the very reason that his power emanates from Kim Il-sung.

Even under the best of circumstances, therefore, Kim Jong-il's chances of sustaining a firm grip on power are limited. Although it is difficult at this stage to forecast the likely make-up of a post-Kim Jong-il leadership, some form of collective ruling body is the most likely, with the military assuming a central position in the power fulcrum. But given that the overall economic situation is likely to decline even further, Pyongyang will have seriously to reconsider its options and eventually reach a political settlement with Seoul.

Under such a scenario, South Korea should earnestly begin to consider a mini-Marshall Plan, although this task will be even more difficult than it was with Germany. Unification costs are sketchy, but various estimates have shown that it will generally run between $250bn and $450bn over a ten-year period. To manage the twin challenge of political change in North Korea with the burden imposed by unification will be South Korea's main task in the 1990s.

Beyond the all-important unification issue, two other challenges confront South Korea. First, on the basis of change which has already transpired around the Korean peninsula, coupled with new responsibilities in the post-unification era, omni-directional foreign policy (*jeonbang waekyo*) should be emphasized in the years ahead. More than ever, 'front-line diplomacy' will assume a key role in sustaining Korea's security interests with the major regional powers, with one qualification.

While South Korea should strive to strengthen its ties with the regional powers, unification must be achieved without their intervention. It has been suggested both in the United States and even in Japan that some form of 'Two Plus Four' model could be introduced in the Korean peninsula.[34] Nevertheless, none of the four major regional powers have any legal justification for participating in the Korean reunification process. To be sure, treaties which are currently in force between the two Koreas and the regional powers may have to be modified after unification, and the UN Security Council will be partially involved insofar as deactivating the UN Command and the Military Armistice Commission is concerned. However, the central point remains that Korean unification is a Korean issue, and the 'Two Plus Four' mechanism cannot be applied in this context.

Second, South Korea's armed forces should be restructured to emphasize its air and sea-lane defence capabilities. Such a task will be even more critical in the post-unification era, although complications will undoubtedly arise in the context of demobilizing North Korea's formidable forces, problems associated with integration and doctrinal adjustments which have to be made by South Korea's national forces. Nevertheless, land-based defence in the post-unification era cannot be sustained strategically or even financially.

Last but not least, South Korea must also reconsider the longer-term viability of formal and informal security mechanisms. While the US–Korea alliance has preserved peace and stability in the Korean peninsula for nearly five decades, efforts to 'Koreanize' Korean security should be stressed more forcefully in the future.[35] In combination with the omni-directional foreign policy noted above, South Korea should also elevate the ongoing trilateral security dialogue among Korea, the United States and Japan. Although it is virtually impossible to envision any wide-ranging security cooperation between Korea and Japan along the lines of the Franco-German model, it would serve the longer-term interests of Seoul and Tokyo in fostering a relationship beyond a zero-sum framework.

Such a transformation, however, must be premised on Japan's assumption of moral responsibility and leadership, coupled with firm political assurances that it will not attempt to disrupt the regional status quo. But if the two countries across the Korea Strait can overcome their differences and form a more enduring relationship, both parties will gain. This is particularly so since 'future Korean strategic policy will be driven, not by artificial divisions and alliances of the Cold War but by the re-emergent realities of geopolitics'.[36]

Conclusion

The basic premise of this paper has been twofold. First, that despite the opportunities tendered by the end of the Cold War, the net impact on North-east Asia has been limited and regional tensions may be on the rise as a result of deeply entrenched national rivalries and the uncertainties associated with great-power strategies. Second, while the search for a common or collective security regime is an admirable one, it confronts a multitude of challenges, at least in the present decade, so that readjustments, when they take place, are more likely in the bilateral context.

While it is tempting to restructure Asian security along European lines, no two North-east Asian powers for the time being are likely to engage in joint security cooperation comparable to the Franco-German experience in Europe. Ironically, the only actor which has been able to sustain a role as a unifier is also the only extraregional power, the United States. But even here, the United States' leverage is likely to decline over the years as its forward-deployed presence decreases commensurate with the increasing voice of other Asian powers. For the time being, no viable option exists other than a creative process of muddling through. In part, such a prognosis rests on the assumption that domestic issues and national strategies will receive more attention in the post-Cold War era, particularly in relation to the political transitions in China and North Korea and the articulation of a more indigenous security posture on the part of Japan, China and even Korea. Moreover, transformations in Indochina, selective political change in South-east Asia, unresolved territorial disputes, as well as pent-up national aspirations, significantly curtail the prospects for a common security outlook.

Over time the diffusion of national tensions will receive higher priority, particularly if the probability of armed conflict increases substantially, for example in the South China Sea. While this is a key challenge for Asia as a whole, its immediate response is likely to focus on maintaining national deterrent strategies.

Notes

[1] The term 'common security' is used here to describe the implementation of non-offensive defence strategies, cooperation with adversaries, the incorporation of non-military factors into security, and collective security mechanisms through such organizations as the United Nations. For a comprehensive review of the roots of common security as applied to the European context with lessons for Asia, see Geoffrey Wiseman, 'Common Security in the Asia–Pacific Region', *The Pacific Review*, vol. 5, no. 1, Spring 1992, especially pp. 42–43 and 49–51.

[2] For instance, see Thomas J. Hirschfield, 'Building Confidence in Korea: The Arms Control Dimension', *The Korean Journal of Defense Analysis*, vol. 4, no. 1, Summer 1992, pp. 23–56, and Banning N. Garrett, 'Ending the US–Soviet Cold War in East Asia: Prospects for Changing Military Strategies', *The Washington Quarterly*, vol. 14, no. 2, Spring 1991, pp. 163–78.

[3] This is not to say that no progress has been made. President George Bush's theatre nuclear arms control initiative of 27 September 1991, coupled with the North–South denuclearization statement of 31 December 1991, could not have been considered without the global end of the Cold War. Nevertheless, other threats have yet to be resolved, such as North Korea's potential nuclear weapons development programme.

[4] Beyond APEC, the ASEAN Post-Ministerial Conference comes closest to resembling a multilateral security dialogue. During the PMC meeting in Manila on 25 July 1992, South Korea's Foreign Minister, Lee Sang-ock, noted that 'as regional exchanges intensify and become more complex, the need for regional security consultations can no longer be neglected. We believe that it is time to study ways to develop security dialogue for the Asia–Pacific region as a measure to enhance confidence and dissipate possible tensions' (ASEAN–Republic of Korea Dialogue session of the ASEAN Post-Ministerial Conference, Manila, 25 July 1992, p. 3).

[5] Laurence Martin, 'National Security in a New World Order', *The World Today*, vol. 48, no. 2, February 1992, p. 26.

[6] John Lewis Gaddis defines the post-Second World War era as one of a 'long peace' in that while not designed to last very long, it 'has now survived twice as long as the far more carefully designed World War I settlement'. See Gaddis, 'The Long Peace: Elements of Stability in the Postwar International System', in

Sean M. Lynn-Jones (ed.), *The Cold War and After: Prospects for Peace* (Cambridge, MA: MIT Press, 1991), pp. 1–2.

[7] For instance, Beijing most recently concluded the first Sino-Indian defence ministers' meeting since 1969. It has also exchanged trade missions with South Korea and established diplomatic relations with Saudi Arabia.

[8] See, for instance, Paul Kennedy, *The Rise and Fall of Great Powers: Economic Change and Military Conflict from 1500 to 2000* (New York: Random House, 1987), especially pp. 517–22 on the future prospects for US involvement in East Asia.

[9] The PKO Bill was first introduced in autumn 1990, but was withdrawn after sustained opposition by the Japanese Socialist Party. The revised bill was finally passed in the Lower House of the Japanese Diet on 15 June 1992 by a vote of 329 to 17, although 137 members of the JSP resigned their parliamentary seats and refused to partake in the vote; see *Chosun-Ilbo*, 16 June 1992. For a Japanese perspective on the PKO issue, see Takashi Inoguchi, 'A Job for the Men from the PKO', *Far Eastern Economic Review*, vol. 150, no. 50, 13 December 1990, p. 23, and Mashashi Nishihara, 'Japan's PKO Law Heralds a Healthy New Era', *Asian Wall Street Journal*, 17 June 1992.

[10] Ironically, the intense pressure which was put on Japan after the Gulf War contributed directly to Tokyo's search for a more viable security role, including the push for some form of multilateral security dialogue within the region, sustained modernization funds for the SDF and its decision to participate in UN peacekeeping operations in Cambodia. See Robert Delfs, 'Offshore Samurai', *Far Eastern Economic Review*, vol. 155, no. 24, 18 June 1992, p. 10.

[11] For example, see Doug Bandow, 'Unfreezing Korea', *The National Interest*, no. 25, Autumn 1991, pp. 51–58.

[12] The official title of this April 1990 report is *A Strategic Framework for the Asia–Pacific Rim: Looking Toward the 21st Century* (Washington, DC: Government Printing Office, 1990). See also US Congress, House of Representatives, 'Statement of the Secretary of Defense

Dick Cheney Before the House Foreign Affairs Committee', 4 March 1992. The 'Defense Planning Guideline for Fiscal Years 1994–1999' originally included passages which spoke of deterring 'other competitors from even aspiring to a larger' role, but the revised version – which has not been made public – has instead focused on the need for 'sustained cooperation among major democratic powers' since the end of the Second World War. See Barton Gellman, 'For Pentagon, Thwarting New Rivals is No Longer Primary Aim', *International Herald Tribune*, 25 May 1992.

[13] Michael Vatikiotis, 'Permanent Presence', *Far Eastern Economic Review*, vol. 155, no. 2, 16 January 1992, p. 22.

[14] *Ibid.*

[15] 'America Isn't Asia's Cop', *New York Times*, 8 August 1992, emphasis added.

[16] Roger W. Sullivan, 'Discarding the China Card', *Foreign Policy*, no. 86, Spring 1992, p. 4.

[17] L.R. Vasey, James A. Kelly and Norman Levin, *Strategic Change in East Asia: A New US Approach* (Honolulu, HI: Pacific Forum/CSIS, January 1992), pp. 17–18, emphasis added.

[18] Gerald Segal, 'Opening and Dividing China', *The World Today*, vol. 48, no. 5, May 1992, p. 78.

[19] As reported in *Chosun-Ilbo*, 21 March 1992.

[20] Nicholas D. Kristof, 'Beijing Continues Military Buildup', *New York Times*, 24 April 1992, reprinted in *The Korea Herald*, 24 April 1992.

[21] For example, Russia recently concluded the transfer of 24 Su-27 warplanes, and it has been reported that the Chinese are actively shopping for MiG-31s as well as missile guidance systems and nuclear fusion technology. See Jim Mann, 'China Bent on Acquiring Hi-Tech Russian Weapons', *Los Angeles Times*, 14 July 1992, as reprinted in *The Korea Herald*, 14 July 1992. Other reports have indicated that China is actively looking into purchasing an aircraft carrier from Russia and even Ukraine for the bargain-basement price of around $200m. See Sheryl WuDunn, 'China Shops for Russian Aircraft Carrier', *International Herald Tribune*, 8 June 1992. For an overview of China's

maritime strategy and naval force upgrades, see 'New Ships for the Plan', *Jane's Defence Weekly*, vol. 17, no. 3, 18 January 1992.

[22] Yasuhide Yamanouchi, 'Japan's Security Policy and Arms Control in Northeast Asia', International Institute for Global Peace (IIGP) Policy Paper, no. 60E, October 1991, p. 1.

[23] Tsuneo Akaha, 'Japan's Comprehensive Security Policy', *Asian Survey*, vol. 31, no. 4, April 1991, pp. 324–25.

[24] *Ibid.*, pp. 328–29.

[25] Hiroyuki Kishino, 'Creating a Japan–US Global Partnership: Japan's Role in a Changing World', IIGP Policy Paper, no. 68E, September 1991, pp. 8–9, emphasis added.

[26] Alan D. Romberg and Marshall M. Bouton, 'The US and Asia in 1991', *Asian Survey*, vol. 32, no. 1, January 1992, p. 3.

[27] US officials have stressed that Washington clearly does not envision any rapid or significant drawdown in its military presence from North-east Asia. The US Ambassador to Tokyo, Michael Armacost, stated in an interview that 'I wouldn't see dramatic changes in the short term . . . A dramatic improvement of the situation in Korea would be the most important single event that would bear on forward deployments in North-east Asia' (*The Korea Herald*, 30 April 1992).

[28] Cited in David E. Sanger, 'Cold War Over, Japan Seeks to Define its Role', *International Herald Tribune*, 6 May 1992.

[29] 'Strong Basis, Strong Future', *Jane's Defence Weekly*, 17 August 1991, p. 276, and 'Blue Water Ambition', *ibid.*, p. 278.

[30] Interview in *Chosun-Ilbo*, 21 June 1992.

[31] Speech by Prime Minister Kiichi Miyazawa at the National Press Club, 2 July 1992, pp. 3, 8, emphasis added.

[32] For an interesting 'look into the future' on the Korean peninsula, see Aidan Foster-Carter, *Korea's Coming Reunification: Another East Asian Superpower?* (London: The Economist Intelligence Unit, April 1992).

[33] According to Lee Choon-kun at the Sejong Institute, North Korea began a concerted defence build-up during the period of global détente (i.e., of improved US–Soviet relations from 1986 until the present). He argues that contrary to Seoul's initial objective of extending its leverage over North Korea through establishing official ties with the Soviet Union, it had the opposite effect and may even have compelled the North Koreans to search for a security 'equalizer' such as an indigenous nuclear weapons capability. For recent information on the North–South military balance, see *Defense White Paper, 1991-1992* (Seoul: Ministry of National Defense, 1992), and *North Korea: The Foundations of Military Strength* (Washington, DC: Defense Intelligence Agency, November 1991), especially Ch. 5.

[34] For example, former US Secretary of State James Baker stated that 'as the North–South dialogue progresses, we [the United States] will explore the possibilities for a forum for the two Koreas and the four major powers in Northeast Asia that will support the dialogue, help in the easing of tensions, facilitate discussion of common security concerns, and *possibly guarantee outcomes negotiated between the two Koreas'*. James A. Baker, III, 'America in Asia: Emerging Architecture for a Pacific Community', *Foreign Affairs*, vol. 70, no. 5, Winter 1991–92, p. 13, emphasis added.

[35] Specifically, operational control should be transferred fully to the Republic of Korea (ROK) in the short to mid-term. Moreover, defence technology transfers should be broadened to increase procurement options for the ROK armed forces.

[36] Foster-Carter, *op. cit.* in note 32, p. 115.

Russia and Other Independent Republics in Asia

DR SERGEI A. KARAGANOV

The recent avalanche-like changes in the former USSR were so swift and unexpected that most analysts and policy-makers are still unable to comprehend the geopolitical implications of the dissolution of the Soviet Union. Usually geopolitical shifts of such magnitude take dozens of years, if not centuries, to work through. Consequently, wars are currently being waged in the region which will lead to the formation of new boundaries, new states and new balances.

Under the pressure of these new realities, strategic analysis is rapidly becoming less of a science and is moving towards becoming something not necessarily less prestigious, but different – an art. Intuition, an awareness of the general history of countries, peoples and religions, and of political psychology, are becoming as useful to strategic analysts as a knowledge of military and economic potentials, the foreign policy orientations of the elite and so on.[1] Most of the factors influencing the situation in the former Soviet Union are either intangible or in a state of flux. The proper 'scientific' tools for assessing it are probably now in the hands of historians of previous centuries or of students of geopolitics, since there is a very real possibility that past history may repeat itself in Eurasia, except in its north-western periphery – western Europe. Of course, such a prediction may prove too pessimistic. However, policies which do not take into consideration worst-case scenarios are usually doomed to failure. In fact, the pessimistic predictions of what could happen in terms of security after the disintegration of the Soviet Union are proving to be largely (though not wholly) true.

The task of analysing the strategic implications (including those for Asia) of the processes in train on the territory of the former Soviet Union, complex in itself, is almost impossible without a prior attempt to create some frame of reference in an inherently unpredictable and fluid situation. In order to predict Russian policy towards Asia, one has at least to try to understand what is and will be Russia, and thus to assess the consequences of what has happened and what might happen to it.

It is widely assumed both within Russia and without that it is a scaled down version of the Russian Tzardom of the sixteenth and seventeenth centuries, of the Russian Empire of the eighteenth to twentieth centuries and of the former Soviet Union – and the true heir to all of them. This is only partly correct. Russia has never existed within the borders it inherited after the dissolution of the Union. While on the geopolitical map it looks almost the same, occupying four-fifths of the territory of the former USSR, it retains little more than 50% of its population and (with the downfall of the economy) less than half the gross national product of the USSR in 1990. By the majority of parameters (excluding territory and nuclear potential) Russia has moved to the category of a medium-sized power. This fact alone is drastically changing not only global constellations, but also the continental balance in Asia.

Russia inherited, in terms of figures, a large proportion of the Soviet military machine. But the overall crisis of state and the necessity of adapting to the partial disintegration of Soviet forces has rendered this machine virtually unusable for major operations, at least for several years. Thus, in addition to the shift in the political and economic balance, a drastic change in the military balance has taken place. (The notion of balance is used here not in its outdated and largely artificial Europe-related sense – as a relatively stable equilibrium of forces – but in its more general sense.)

In Asia, these changes are occurring against the backdrop of a continent where, contrary to the global tendency towards a relative decline in the usefulness of force, military force in its politically sophisticated – and even in its simple – forms is still playing its traditional role. This is especially true for the regions of Southern and Central Asia, where a group of states is living through a stage of history, and of socio-economic and political development, that can be compared (though, of course, it is in many ways different) to the Europe of the late nineteenth and early twentieth centuries – the stage of early imperialism, in the old Marxist parlance.

It is highly unlikely that these expansionist and/or imperial aspirations would be directed against Russia proper. Russia is still too strong for such attempts and possesses nuclear weapons which simply rule out, at least for the time being, any direct conflict. Russia is also now separated from this region by a group of new, though weak, states – the former republics of the Soviet Union. Thus, 'the Southern threat', widely discussed in Moscow, is grossly overvalued.

But how the dark military shadow of the mighty USSR has been influencing the behaviour of these states towards each other is still unknown. Could the weakening of Russia create a vacuum which would help unfreeze some of these conflicts, for instance, by strengthening forces in Pakistan which are hostile to India, a long-time geostrategic ally of the USSR? In this area, however, the overall implications of the demise of the Soviet Union are relatively unclear and should not cause acute concern, particularly because the potential vacuum has been filled by the psychological consequences of the defeat of Iraqi aggression, and by attempts to demonstrate the effectiveness of internationally sponsored coalitions in cases of necessity.

Another possible and further-reaching consequence of the disintegration of the USSR and the current relative weakness of Russia is the new role of China. While its northern counterpart has lost a large part of its political, economic and military power, China's geopolitical status has altered to the extent that it could even be seen as the potential dominating power in continental Asia.

This is not to call into question the current foreign policy of the Chinese leadership, which is mostly responsible and cautious. However, it is necessary to keep in mind future possibilities, for example the destabilization of the process of reform in China, the radicalization of its leadership or, on the road to capitalism, its acquisition of some of the traits of an imperialist power.

The possible new geopolitical role of China has to be thoroughly assessed, and new policies to cope with it should be developed both by the Chinese leadership and by the international community. Otherwise China could in the future occupy a place somewhat similar to that previously occupied by the Soviet Union – that of a perceived massive threat to all its neighbours.

Another significant, but less dramatic, consequence of the demise of the USSR is the obvious accelerated increase not only in the economic, but also in the political – and probably politico-military – weight of Japan. The need for Japan to seek the protection of its transpacific ally, and to pay the political price for this protection, is gradually declining. Coupled with the piecemeal (and unfortunate) withdrawal of the United States from the area, the increasing influence of Japan is not only causing concern among Association of South-East Asian Nations (ASEAN) countries, but could also potentially place Japan on a collision course with China.

Much in Asia, as well as elsewhere, will depend on the kind of political future the Russian leadership chooses, or is made to choose, by social and political forces beyond its control. In principle there are three major scenarios which could develop in Russia: the relatively smooth, decade-long creation of a base for a modern market economy and for a democratic political system; neo-totalitarian (neo-fascist) degeneration and almost inevitable disintegration; or evolution between these two extremes.

The 'democratic market' scenario would most probably strengthen the pro-Western and pro-European orientation of Russia, and would eventually do away with most of the barriers dividing it from the Atlantic Community. The Vancouver to Tokyo strategic alliance – a robust foundation for global and Asian stability – could soon become a reality. The creation of such a pillar of stability would probably prevent or ameliorate a repetition of past history in most of the landmass of Eurasia. Many of the potential dangers would be deterred, and instability in Central and Southern Asia could be prevented from escalating both vertically and horizontally. The growth of China under these circumstances would cause much less concern among its neighbours. Obviously this scenario is the most benign. Unfortunately, due to the speed of development, the depth of the crisis, the cultural predispositions and traditions of the population and – above all – to the tensions brought about by the disintegration of the Soviet Union, this scenario is not the most probable one.

A totalitarian backlash, producing a hostile encirclement of the West, would not push the leaders of such a coup into an alliance with Asia as a whole, but with the less democratic and responsible regimes in Asia: first with Iraq and North Korea; and then, probably, with Iran. However, a close alliance with the latter could not last very long, given the vast cultural and religious differences, as well as the probable tensions that would emerge over attempts to take back full control of the Asian republics of the former USSR. But in any event the most radical, anti-Western and anti-democratic forces in Asia would gain a relatively powerful ally. Such a regime would probably attempt to forge an anti-Western alliance with China, too. But, if previously cautious Chinese diplomacy can be used as a yardstick for the behaviour of Beijing, the Chinese will refrain from such an alliance. What is more, this would be an alliance with a weak and poor partner against mighty and affluent countries. Overall, such a scenario would significantly strengthen stability in Asia, but would not endanger the global status quo dramatically.

On the other hand, a totalitarian coup would most probably be just a short cut towards either the disintegration of Russia and the creation on the territory of the Russian Federation of several fully independent quasi-states, or the dissolution of the Federation, or the secession from it of major territories. This could also happen by default as a result of the inaction or mistakes of the current leadership.

If disintegration takes place and several quasi-states begin to form on Russian territory, and if the Russian leadership still retains some instinct for self-preservation, it would provoke a forceful reaction, which, if relatively successful, would bring to power a nationalist–authoritarian regime and place Russia in a position of semi-isolation. If such an attempt were to fail, low-intensity civil war would break out, accelerating the disintegration of the armed forces. Many consequences, including the loss of control over weapons of mass destruction, would follow. For Asia, this would mean total withdrawal of the remainder of Russia from any constructive role in the republics of Central Asia. Weak quasi-states, which could be formed, for example in Siberia and the Russian Far East, would literally suck in outside interference and even interventions – some of them of a new 'non-belligerent' type – in order to secure control over weapons of mass destruction. And more disasters resulting from this chaos could be enumerated. But the conclusion would be the same. If there is now a tendency towards the creation of a 'geostrategic hole' on the territory of the former Soviet Union, the disintegration of Russia would create an abyss – a totally unregulated security space in the centre of Eurasia drawing in outside powers and spreading out instability. Instead of the 'new world order', history in its ugliest forms would return to most of Eurasia. This 'hole' is currently obvious in the Caucasus, which has been profoundly – for years and, more likely, decades – destabilized in and around Moldova. In other places there exists only the potential for the creation of such a 'hole', and not yet the reality.

The third, most probable, scenario of the development of Russia in the foreseeable future is a gradual, though uneven, evolution of the country towards modernity. That evolution will take at least a quarter of a century. Politically it would be a semi-authoritarian, semi-democratic state, with state–capitalist structures dominant in the economy and a gradually growing, genuinely private sector. The new ruling elite – managers of state and partly privatized state enterprises, new private entrepreneurs and representatives of the army, police and internal security – would not be interested in a total economic and political opening-up to the West, since this could endanger some of their political and economic interests. At the same time, this ruling elite in its absolute majority would be deeply interested in close cooperation with the developed world, and would understand that its well-being was heavily dependent on such cooperation.

A semi-democratic political system, periods of authoritarian politics, strained relations with neighbours and even the temporary return of neo-imperial ambitions would most probably slow down strategic *rapprochement* with the West, even if cooperative elements in relations were to prevail.

A close alliance with the West could be hindered or postponed by its inability and, to some extent, unwillingness to provide substantial aid, by its doubts over whether it wants the resurrection of a politically strong Russia or not, and by its preoccupation with its own internal agenda. Because of this inability and doubt, Russia must rely first of all on its own efforts to modernize itself.

Thus the one-sided Western (or rather American) orientation of Russian foreign policy in the first months after the creation of the new Russia in August 1991 was objectively doomed. The somewhat apprentice-like manner in which this diplomacy was conducted only speeded up the growth of opposition towards this Western orientation. On the surface this opposition was created by anti-democratic and anti-Western disciples of communists and by ultra-conservative isolationists. However, the opposition ran much deeper. It had its roots in the core national interests of Russia and in the understanding, even of the pro-Western elite, that a one-sided orientation towards the West was futile, and in the disappointment of such an elite at the modest character of Western aid. This disappointment was also partly born of too high expectations.

Political and economic limitations, which would slow down *rapprochement* with the West, are already inevitably pushing Russia towards a more even-handed approach to Asia (and to the Third World to which politically, as well as economically, Russia partly belongs). However, under relatively normal circumstances this would not call into question the long-term orientation towards a strategic alliance with the West, without which Russia will be hardly able to defend its core security and geopolitical interests in the twenty-first century. The necessity for partial reorientation towards Asia and some of the Third World nations also has its roots in Russia's economic interests. Most of its manufactured goods have little chance of penetrating Western markets. The only ones that have – armaments and aerospace products – are being blocked from entering the Western market. This policy is short sighted and counter productive. Instead of being co-opted and integrated, the powerful political and economic interests connected with the Russian armaments industry are being pushed in an anti-Western direction. A side effect of these policies will be, of course, a further shift towards relatively indiscriminate arms sales to almost any potential client (except for two or three of the most obviously dangerous) in the South, and particularly to China.

Another factor which pushes Russia economically towards Asia is the relative depletion of its oil resources due to the inadequacy and obsolescence of the technology of extraction and transportation. If not corrected by massive investment, one of the few life-lines connecting Russia with Europe and generating vital income to fund imports from Europe will be cut off.

Partial economic reorientation towards such countries as China, South Korea, Pakistan, Iran, Saudi Arabia and other Gulf countries and ASEAN states, as well as the resurrection of traditional ties with Syria and India, will call for a less Western-oriented foreign policy. This would strengthen the bargaining position of these states in the world community. Such a reorientation towards Asia would be encouraged by the fact that the political and economic weight of Russian Siberia and the Russian Far East could become relatively greater in Russia than it was in the former Soviet Union.

The middle-of-the-road model of development, envisaged in this paper for Russia, would include the continuation of the relative decentralization of economic activities. Regions will continue to acquire more rights *vis-à-vis* foreign trade and consular and other relations with neighbouring countries and regions, particularly with Japan, both Koreas, China and Mongolia. This tendency towards transborder regionalization reflects a worldwide tendency and is largely healthy. In the case of Russia it also means the return to the *status quo ante*, to the situation which traditionally existed in 'old' Russia in which regions and their governors had a great deal of independence in their relations with their neighbours. Overcentralization, when all activities were put under the close surveillance and control of the Moscow government, was a Soviet departure from a two-centuries-old tradition. This regionalization could create problems only if it becomes an additional incentive for secession, or if the deep economic involvement of neighbouring countries recreates a basis for territorial claims. Regionalization will also mean that the Moscow government, conducting its grand strategy, will have to take into consideration regional interests. Hopefully the lessons of Sakhalin's opposition on the Kuril Islands issue will remind Moscow bureaucracies of the necessity of consulting with regions and political groups before formulating a policy, rather than after the event.

The inevitable turn towards a more active and constructive engagement in Asia is a result of the growing understanding of the Russian elite that a country which is 8% Muslim and borders the Muslim world cannot afford to be negligent of or hostile towards Islam. This change is also prompted by the emerging realization that Islam is not as big a threat to Russian interests as had previously been presumed due to a lack of specific knowledge of the situation as well as the indiscriminate embrace by some politically influential intellectuals of the more alarmist views of Islam emanating from the West, particularly from the United States.

This change of direction towards Asia is also prompted by the realization that Russia – despite alleged cultural and political backwardness and the relatively low level of economic development of most of the former Soviet Asian republics – must not shy away from its responsibility for what is happening in the former Asian republics of the Soviet Union. It is becoming evident that the long-term costs of such a retreat could become much greater than any short-term benefits, and that even those are largely elusive.

The growth of interest in the Asian republics was brought about by the understanding that a potentially dangerous vacuum of at least two types could be created in the area. The first is relatively obvious. These states could become the targets of their southern neighbours not only for political, economic, religious and cultural expansion (which has already started and is in a way inevitable), but also for military-political and even purely military expansion. There are already some signs of that, especially on the Afghan border.

Some countries in the area are also concerned about possible border problems with China. While the Soviet government managed to solve almost all of the contentious border issues between China and the Russian Federation, similar work on the borders between Kazakhstan, Kyrgyzstan and Tajikistan has yet to be done.

The vacuum of the second type is potentially more dangerous. Most of the states in the area are not only poor, but also have almost completely artificial borders with little historic legitimacy. The borders of the republics, which were created after the 1917 revolution, largely resemble those drawn by the colonial powers in Africa. Most countries are suffering from overpopulation and are multinational.

Usually only the so-called Russian minority is mentioned as a potential problem in this context. But virtually each of the republics has several sizeable minorities. Suppression of one of them could bring about a chain reaction, throwing the whole region into chaos, creating uncontrollable migrations, flows of refugees and spreading instability to the nearby areas of Russia. Russia cannot afford such a development, particularly for economic reasons. Several branches of industry in Russia are dependent on raw materials and spare parts produced in the area and, above all, on cotton, which, if bought on the world market, would prove much more expensive.

Also, many observers are afraid that the competition between Iran, Turkey, Pakistan and Saudi Arabia for influence in the former Soviet republics of Asia will bring Islamic fundamentalism into the region. However, these fears are most probably exaggerated. The Shi'ites are in a tiny minority in the area. So far nationalism and not religion is dominating the political scene of the new countries, and most of those competing for influence are not fundamentalist.

A realization of the factors involved is moving Russian Asian policy in a conservative direction. Moscow is starting to understand that democracy has no immediate future in most of the republics, and that the opposition, if it comes to power, will not bring democracy, but rather more radical nationalism, destabilization and chaos, providing fertile ground for the growth of religious fundamentalism in the future. Now evolving Russian policies are thoroughly realist; they support the status quo and the stability of regimes rather than ideological predispositions. The earlier passivity is gradually being replaced. But the reinvolvement of Moscow is not absolute. It concentrates first of all on economic and politico-military aspects where mutual interests are obvious.

The closest ties, indeed possibly a close alliance, is being recreated with Kazakhstan – a country half-Asian, half-European and in many ways resembling an Asian version of Russia itself. Kazakhstan, less unstable than other republics, could prove to be a valuable ally in regulating turmoil in Central Asia.

This support of status-quo policies has its weakness of course: that it does not side with the forces of change which could eventually come to power. But experience with the destabilizing consequences of change in the former USSR and the situation in Afghanistan, where withdrawal of support for Najibullah brought only a massive flare-up of the civil war, pushes Moscow towards more conservative and cautious policies.

The partial recognition by Moscow of the importance of former Soviet Central Asia is prompted also by movement from the other side. After enjoying for some time their newly and unexpectedly acquired independence, most Central Asian leaders have realized that Turkey or Saudi Arabia can provide aid and political support, but are not markets for traditional exports. Indeed, an expansion of trade in the area is a non-starter (Kazakhstan and Uzbekistan have already rejected proposals for the creation of an economic union of former Soviet Central Asian states). But above all, they understand that nobody except for Russia can guarantee their borders and, to a certain degree, even the viability of their regimes. These kinds of considerations received an additional impetus after the violent but temporary overthrow of the leadership of Tajikistan in May 1992.

Thus the Central Asian states are generally supportive of the creation of viable Commonwealth of Independent States (CIS) structures and are refraining from the forceful nationalization of military forces on their territory. Most are ready for military ties with Russia. It seems that a new mutually acceptable balance is being achieved: independence, but close integration with Russia, from the Asian states' perspective; integration and limited involvement in key areas from the Russian perspective. The growing influence of Turkey and Iran is watched with some concern, but also with relative nonchalance. Analysts believe that competition between several outside powers provides Russia with additional room for manoeuvre. This competition is also taking some of the potential economic burden off Russian shoulders.

It is clear that the balance which is being achieved is extremely fragile and that the area has more sources of profound destabilization, territorial reshuffling and conflicts than any other area in the former Soviet Union except for the Caucasus. However, the partial post-imperial resurgence of Russia, which may already be occurring, could provide some guarantee against the escalation of conflicts and the deterioration of the area into a 'black hole'. It is also obvious that Russia can neither afford, nor is willing, to be the sole guarantor of stability; therefore international structures, first of all the Conference on Security and Cooperation in Europe (CSCE) and the North Atlantic Cooperation Council (NACC), but also regional Asian structures, should be used to create a system for the prevention and regulation of conflicts in the region. Even more promising would be bilateral Russian–Turkish cooperation on these matters. However, it is unclear whether such cooperation could be forged.

At the same time this shift towards Asia has obvious limitations. Most of the economic and political interests of Russia still lie in the West. While making Russia less European geographically and economically, the disintegration of the USSR made it more European culturally and politically. The drive towards Asia is also hindered by the relatively modest prospects of *rapprochement* with Japan – both due to the territorial issue, and to the relatively low interest of Japanese business in the development of the Russian Far East.

The investment of goodwill, which has recently been made by the West, and the obvious absence of a threat from the West, will also mean that a partial turn to Asia would not constitute a retreat from the West or a return to anti-Western policies, but will lead instead to a more balanced policy orientation. A lot, of course, will also depend on the policies of the West.

Russian Asian policy has yet to be formulated. Some of its possible elements have been described, many are still unclear – and the bureaucratic chaos in Moscow could delay its ultimate formulation. However if this structural ineptitude is overcome, there is a real chance that Russia will have an Asian policy. Previously lofty declarations – be they in Vladivostok or in Krasnoyarsk – about Russia turning to Asia inevitably ended with Moscow's policies concentrating on Washington or, and to a lesser extent, on European capitals.

With new geopolitics, new challenges and a new weakness, Russia cannot afford to continue the benevolent negligence which characterized Soviet Asian policies for decades. But its policy should, of course, be part and parcel of a wider strategy. The long-term goal of this strategy should be the creation of a strategic alliance with the West, including the Western-oriented Asian countries on the perimeter of Russia, an alliance embracing the space from Vancouver to Tokyo or Seoul, an alliance not aimed against anybody, any country or any religion, but against instability, aggression and aggressive nationalism.

This alliance could have a military dimension in which Russia would play a significant role in deterring conflicts in Eurasia. Only such an alliance would lead Russia to the eventual demilitarization of its policies and economy. This alliance, gradually spreading southwards, is the only way of preventing a repetition of history in Eurasia. An alliance with the West which included the developed and democratic countries of the Far East (coupled with good relations with the rest of Asia) would be Russia's only hope of finding a comfortable place in geography and history and to live at peace with itself. Russia is neither fully European nor completely Asian. Born of the historic interaction of the steppes and the forests, of the Bible and the Koran, of Europe and Asia, Russia is both. Recently, Foreign Minister Andrei Kozyrev found an eloquent formula for the new Russian policy: 'We have an unprecedented possibility to be Asians in Asia, Europeans in Europe and democrats in the world'.[2]

That is, of course, a lofty declaration, and the latter part of it contains an element of wishful thinking. But in these dramatic times we should take into consideration not only new dangers, but also new possibilities.

There is one possibility not yet mentioned: Russia now has the chance to demonstrate that the famous Kipling dictum that 'East is East and West is West and never the twain shall meet' was wrong. But it has to prove that, of course.

Notes

[1] For a systematic and eloquent description of some of the problems strategic analysis now faces, see John Chipman, 'The Future of Strategic Studies', *Survival*, vol. 34, Spring 1992, pp. 109–31.

[2] A. Kozyrev, 'Resurrection or a Kafkian Metamorphosis', *Nezavisimaya Gazeta*, 20 August 1992, pp. 1, 4.

Nuclear Proliferation in the Post-Cold War World

AMBASSADOR RYUKICHI IMAI

The role of nuclear weapons was clear, or at least so it appeared, during the forty-five years of East–West confrontation. Various strategic doctrines, as well as the use of tactical weapons, with particular emphasis on the central role of Europe, have been extensively discussed. With the end of the Cold War, justifying the continued existence of nuclear weapons is becoming increasingly difficult. The questions of arms reduction and disposal present problems of unusual gravity, especially in the former Soviet Union where effective control of the vast number of strategic and tactical weapons in the former territory seems to have been lost. This may serve to intensify the already complicated problems of nuclear weapons proliferation in the Third World. It may be useful to remember that the Third World, and especially its non-aligned component, is facing a major identity crisis.

Nuclear weapons proliferation became an important concern in the 1960s when discussion of the 'nth country' problem began. The Atoms for Peace movement, promoted by General Eisenhower's 1953 United Nations speech, presented the irresistible temptation of an 'unlimited supply of energy' in the pre-oil, coal-dependent and energy-short post-war reconstruction period. The Kennedy administration became alarmed at the prospect that nuclear weapons were no longer concentrated in the hands of a chosen few. Anyone with the scientific knowledge and industrial capabilities would be able to become the 'nth country'. This contributed to the conclusion of the 1963 Partial Test Ban Treaty and the 1970 Nuclear Non-Proliferation Treaty (NPT).[1] The NPT focused on the Federal Republic of Germany and Japan, who finally ratified the Treaty in 1975 and 1976, respectively.

The 1977 Carter non-proliferation initiative was prompted by the prospect of the extensive use of plutonium for nuclear fuel, resulting from the rapid growth in nuclear power programmes throughout the world following the 1973 oil crisis. Towards the end of the 1970s, the US government calculated a possible 2.5–3 billion kilowatt capacity for nuclear power generation by the end of the century. The fuel requirement would exceed known uranium resources and enrichment capacities, thus calling for the early commercialization of plutonium fuel. The 1974 Energy Research and Development Agency (ERDA) report urged the increased development of fast breeders.[2] The Carter administration attempted to enforce a worldwide prohibition on commercial plutonium, and in the process ran into trouble with the nuclear programmes of the Federal Republic and Japan. However, the United States was successful in suspending the construction of plutonium-extraction plants, imported from France, in Pakistan and the Republic of Korea. US-initiated international nuclear-fuel cycle evaluation (INFCE) was of no real consequence. With decreasing oil prices and increasing alarm over safety, the world lost interest in nuclear power. The Mexican debt crisis of 1972 and the 1976 decrease in oil prices had their effects, and the Three Mile Island power station accident of 1979 made the point even more sharply. As of 1992, the expected capacity for nuclear power generation by the end of the century is about 400m kilowatts.

The 1990s have witnessed open challenges to the international non-proliferation regime in the form of Iraqi and North Korean reluctance to enter into a safeguards agreement with the International Atomic Energy Agency (IAEA). The 1970 IAEA safeguards, in accordance with Article 3 of the NPT, are based on statistical samplings of nuclear materials accounting and are designed to provide for the timely detection of the diversion of more than significant quantities of material unaccounted for (MUF).[3] The safeguards are built on mutual confidence and rely on countries making available information about their nuclear materials and facilities. The agreement provides for unscheduled special inspections of undeclared facilities. The safeguards system, however, is not intended to counter those who may conduct nuclear weapons activities with an undeclared fuel cycle. The UN Special Commission, under Security Council Resolution 687, discovered that Iraq had been conducting uranium mining, enrichment and metal fabrication on a very large scale outside the declared Twaitha Research Center, which had been subject to IAEA inspections. It was only because of a timely coincidence that these weapons activities became known to the United Nations. Someone closely involved in the Iraqi weapons programme personally took action to inform the UN investigation team, and the subsequent visiting UN team was fired at by Iraqi guards. The international community cannot expect this type of fortuitous coincidence to occur in every case of clandestine weapons activity.

The case of North Korea is more difficult because the country is even more intractable than Iraq. For some time North Korea has been operating a Calder Hall-type gas-cooled graphite reactor with an electrical output of 5MWe. This is an ideal instrument with which to produce weapons-grade plutonium rich in Pu^{239} isotopes. North Korea is also operating a radio-chemical laboratory which looks very like a plutonium separation plant. Another reactor is under construction, and three large power stations, probably of Soviet design, are reportedly under consideration. Until the IAEA has more detailed access to these and other (possibly undeclared) facilities, it is difficult to assess the scale of their activities and whether a plutonium implosion-type atomic bomb is a possibility. The fact that North Korea delayed signing the IAEA agreement by asking for the withdrawal of US tactical warheads in the Republic of Korea (which they have inadvertently achieved), and the fact that there was worldwide press coverage about the Korean bomb, may have led Pyongyang to believe that it is using the nuclear card successfully.

It has never been clear whether either or both of the former super-powers could have started an all-out intercontinental ballistic missile (ICBM) attack on the other for various reasons. Liquid-fuelled SS-18s are extremely difficult to keep on alert all the time; disturbance from the gravity field near the North Pole alone could have confused actual targeting accuracy; it would have taken some time before the respective communication links of Moscow and Washington would have been secure enough to transmit firing orders. Also, it was never clear whether 7,200 or 3,500 tactical weapons in western Europe (and as many nuclear tactical systems in Warsaw Pact countries) could have been justified. In any event, the world was not prepared for the removal of the majority of the warheads from service and for dismantling them in good order.[4]

Warhead transportation, storage and dismantling, as well as the subsequent handling of weapons-grade plutonium and highly enriched uranium, are very complicated and delicate processes, as the US Congress discovered when it appropriated $400m assistance for this purpose out of the 1993 fiscal year defence budget.[5] Three disquieting facts regarding ex-Soviet nuclear activities, both military and civilian, are that protection against low-level radiation is not adequately provided for; a special fissionable material accountancy regime is not operating; and the physical protection of both materials and weapons is unsatisfactory. These are normally considered the three pillars of safe nuclear operations. There is obviously a need to prevent proliferation of 'a few warheads' into the Third World arms market, and to protect against possible attack by terrorists or by parties in civil war. The International Science and Technology Center was established through joint funding by the United States, the European Economic Community (EEC) and Japan to prevent the 'brain drain' of weapons scientists and engineers from warhead laboratories such as Arzamas 16 or Chelyabinsk 70.[6] These are the new and hitherto unexpected aspects of nuclear weapons and technology proliferation.

Technology transfer between the North and South
During the period when East–West nuclear confrontation was the focus of international concern, both the United States and the former Soviet Union took consolidated action to prevent nuclear proliferation in the Third World. Preventing the transfer of sensitive technologies did not seem to raise too many problems among advanced industrialized countries. India and Brazil were the acknowledged champions against the NPT, and consistently criticized the positions of the nuclear weapon states as unfair. It has been customary for this issue to be

repeated at NPT review conferences every five years. The argument usually centres around the nuclear weapon states' obligations under Article 6 to 'pursue negotiations in good faith on effective measures relating to cessation of the nuclear arms race'. Whether the comprehensive test ban (CTB) will be achieved has become the major piece of unfinished business from the 1963 Partial Test Ban Treaty.

The significance of the NPT and CTB debates will be magnified in 1995 because Article 10(ii) specifies that 'twenty-five years after the entry into force of the Treaty, a conference shall be convened to decide whether the Treaty shall continue in force indefinitely, or shall be extended for an additional fixed period or periods. The decision shall be taken by a majority of the Parties to the Treaty'. It is theoretically possible that an extension for a year or less could be agreed on, virtually terminating the NPT and thus bringing the world back to the period when nuclear armament was a legitimate policy option for any sovereign state. A simple majority of some 120 states is a very different situation from previous review conferences in which consensus was required to adopt final declarations. In the UN disarmament process, the customary political groupings have always been the 'Western group', 'socialists' and the 'non-aligned'. On non-proliferation matters, the Western group and socialists usually worked together.[7]

Even after the end of the Cold War, the United States has not changed its view that a CTB is a long-term (and thus not an immediately realizable) objective. President Yeltsin at one point declared the cessation of all nuclear tests, but has reportedly changed his position with regard to the Novaya Zemlya test site in the Barents Sea. The Semipalatinsk test site has been closed by Kazakhstan. Whether Yeltsin's change of mind represents strong pressure from the military still in command of the strategic and tactical nuclear forces is yet to be seen. It is not yet clear who controls all the strategic missiles and their command, control, communications and intelligence (C^3I) as well as the weapons laboratories and production and assembling facilities of the former Soviet Union. The May 1992 Lisbon Protocol, which brought Russia, Ukraine, Byelarus and Kazakhstan together for the Strategic Arms Reduction Talks (START) Treaty seemed to indicate the failure of US attempts to have Russia speak for the entire former Soviet nuclear forces. Whoever may ratify the START Treaty, as well as put in force the Bush–Yeltsin accord of June 1992 to reduce strategic warheads to between 3,000 and 3,500 each (in the process of eliminating all SS-18 ICBMs by the year 2003), would be able to prove or disprove the US long-term position on the need for occasional nuclear tests.

In addition to strengthening the London Guidelines of 1978, there are other technology transfer restraints regarding chemical weapons, biological weapons and missile technologies with ranges over 500 kilometres and throw-weights of more than 300 kilograms.[8] The Chemical Weapons Treaty was signed in January 1993 and requires a different type of management body and international understanding for restraints on technology transfer. The Coordinating Committee for Multilateral Export Controls (COCOM), after 43 years of doubtful eminence, is now seeking new arrangements and a new *raison d'être*. All these are moves in the direction of restraining the transfer of technology from North to South and, like the new international environmental controls, can lead to reactions very different from those of the Cold War era.[9]

According to recent statistics from the US Arms Control and Disarmament Agency, countries in the Middle East in 1989 spent 12.0% of their gross national product (GNP) on military purposes as against 5.8% for the US and 11.7% for the USSR. Per capita military spending was $1,145 for the Middle East, versus $1,222 for the US and $1,077 for the USSR. Although the developing world accounted for only 16.2% of worldwide military expenditure in 1989, 64.5% of the world's armed forces were in the developing world. Of the world's arms imports, 76.4% ($45bn in 1989) was purchased by the developing world (Middle East 26.6%, South Asia 17.4%, East Asia 11.8%, Africa 8.8% and Latin America 5.6%). If the Gulf countries are included in Asia, the Asian proportion becomes very much larger. The developed world (41.4% North Atlantic Treaty Organisation, 47.3% Warsaw Pact) accounted for 90.3% of the military sales. Leading arms importers in 1989 were Saudi Arabia, Afghanistan, India, Greece and Iraq, in that order. Soviet exports were 43.1% and US exports 27.8% of the world total.[10] Controlling North-to-South transfers of weapons (and related technologies) is easier said than done. The conversion of military production facilities to a consumer-oriented economy is proving very difficult in the Soviet Union. There are indications that those in charge may be tempted to continue producing weapons and so earn much-needed foreign exchange. Nor has the United States been a reluctant arms salesman.

Although not large compared to the arms sales of the Soviet Union ($19.6bn in 1989) and the United States ($11.2bn), China ($2bn), Israel ($625m), North Korea ($400m), Egypt ($370m) and Bulgaria ($160m) were the leading arms exporters in the developing world. None of these are members of the arms-transfer-restraining regimes. China is said to have agreed to join the Missile Technology Control Regime (MTCR) and also became a party to the NPT in early 1992. The situation in Bulgaria is difficult to judge because of its continued need for an export market. North Korea has exported missiles to countries such as Iran and Syria, even in early 1992. North Korea's activities in the sale of nuclear (research) technologies are also attracting attention. It may be too early to predict the likely direction of the developing-world arms trade when the arms sales of the United States and the former Soviet Union remain unpredictable.

Also relevant to the future of the world trade system is the outcome of the current round of General Agreement on Tariffs and Trade

(GATT) negotiations, as well as the possible development of the EC and the North American Free Trade Agreement (NAFTA). Depending on their outcome(s), the Asia–Pacific region may have to choose between a loose arrangement, which includes the United States and Canada, like the Asia–Pacific Economic Cooperative (APEC), or the proposed East Asia Economic Caucus (EAEC), which does not include the United States.

The future of nuclear technology in Asia

In 1990, nuclear power provided 51.4% of the total electricity in South Korea, 38.3% in Taiwan, 26.3% in Japan, 20.6% in the US, 14.8% in Canada, 12.5% in the former USSR and 2.2% in India. In Asia, nuclear power is not a negligible factor. On the other hand, North Korea, Iran and Iraq have taken a serious interest in nuclear technology, but have no significant peaceful nuclear activities. The Republic of Korea and Japan, each with more than 40% reliance (of total primary energy) on Gulf oil, have reason to reduce their dependence on oil in favour of the nuclear option.[11]

One important observation in the context of peaceful nuclear power versus nuclear weapons is that of genuine need. Uranium enrichment and plutonium extraction as technologies are common to both power and weapons. In most of the nuclear weapons states, as well as in Germany and Japan, these activities are practised on an industrial scale. Those with large-scale nuclear power projects would wish to possess relevant fuel-cycle technologies, although there may be arguments for and against such technologies. Countries far from the practical use of industrial nuclear energy can hardly claim legitimate interest in enrichment and/or plutonium technologies. These are heavily technological and capital investment-oriented industries, kept secret for fear of weapons proliferation. China, which already possesses nuclear weapons, would have been a very difficult case if it were a non-nuclear weapons state interested in the industrial nuclear fuel cycle. China is operating a 300MWe power plant of its own design, and plans to import more and larger power stations in the future. The Republic of Korea today would qualify for enrichment or fuel reprocessing technologies. But neither it nor Taiwan have indicated any interest in these activities. Japan, on the other hand, has been building up industrial-scale capabilities in both.

Another important distinction, often overlooked or intentionally played down, is the difference between weapons-grade plutonium that is extracted from (mainly natural uranium) short burn-up fuel of 'Pu production reactors', and normal light-water reactor fuel with a burn-up of some 20,000 MWD/Te. The difference is in the isotopic contents of plutonium (93.5% as against 58% of Pu^{239}). It is known that reactor-grade plutonium can also be used for nuclear explosive devices and has been proven to work. However, it is a material that is more difficult to handle, generates more heat and creates more neutron background, and thus a self-initiated chain reaction is more likely to occur. There is a greater uncertainty in predicting yield (or explosive power), and it is more difficult to store for a long time. Given the choice, weapons-grade plutonium is easier to use and a more logical choice. It requires a small reactor, a small-scale plutonium extraction facility and involves shorter fuel burn-up. This then requires more frequent refuelling and is the least economical for power generation. (This is what North Korea has chosen.) There are thus important differences between the plutonium to be shipped back from France and the UK to Japan, and the plutonium to be extracted from US and former Soviet nuclear warheads. Pakistan's way to an Islamic bomb is through centrifuge enrichment technology, which was stolen from the European Joint Centrifuge.

US tactical nuclear weapons have been withdrawn from the Republic of Korea, and those carried by the Seventh Fleet have also been withdrawn. Except for Guam, there are supposed to be no US nuclear weapons in the Asia–Pacific region. It is assumed that the nuclear umbrella will continue to exist in future to make a US presence felt in the still-uncertain Asian power balance. It would require a major change in US foreign policy to announce publicly its discontinuation. What will happen to the weapons in the former Soviet Union is very uncertain. A number of ICBMs are known to have been deployed along the Mongolian border. *Backfire*-mounted air-launched cruise missiles (ALCMs) are based along the Sea of Japan, and submarine-launched ballistic missile (SLBM) submarines were in Petropavlovsk-Kamchatskiy. Tactical air weapons were based in areas from Vladivostok to Sakhalin. Detailed plans for their removal and dismantling have not been made known. Those tactical weapons known to have existed in Kazakhstan and eastern autonomous republics within Russia require special attention, for along with China's weapons they could lead to a new kind of regional balance devoid of doctrinal justification. If Russia wishes to receive financial and technical assistance from the outside world, the location of weapons and proposed disposal details should be reported to the international community.

China after Deng Xiaoping is difficult to predict. There are even those who foresee a possible federation composed of the North-east, Beijing, Guangdong, Tibet, Inner Mongolia and the Central Asian Muslim republics. What will happen to China's nuclear forces is uncertain even without such extreme scenarios. The Islamic region, extending from the Fertile Crescent through the Central Asia plateau all the way to Indonesia, could conceivably turn both fundamentalist and nuclear. Chinese history is full of examples of powers in outer areas taking control of military strength and establishing autonomous states, with only a CIS-type umbrella left in Beijing. China today may be regretting the help it has given North Korea's nuclear programme. It is possible that China's economic needs would force it to stop the current expansion of its own nuclear arsenal. Not much attention has been given to India's nuclear capability, and India has remained silent since its 1974 underground testing. It has too much to lose by announcing itself nuclear, even as tacitly as Israel did.

Iraq's nuclear programme has led the world to a number of interesting observations in addition to the problem of implementing special inspections (see above). It revealed that there are always businessmen willing to sell sensitive technologies whenever a customer with cash is at hand. A list of the names of those who provided technology, components and other useful information to Iraq was seized by an international team which was prevented by the Baghdad authorities from leaving a car park with the information. The list was not released, but respective governments were informed of the names which led to the update of the London Guidelines in Warsaw in February 1992. Iraq's programme has also underlined the large gap between theoretical knowledge and production know-how. In spite of speculation about how close Saddam Hussein was to possessing a bomb, it is believed that he was still more than a year away from producing a meaningful amount of highly enriched uranium, and several years away from the knowledge of uranium metallurgy necessary for making a 20 kilogramme weapon-shaped core with all the requisite accessories ready for implosion.[12]

The same observations may or may not apply to North Korea. North Korea, as noted above, is one of the leading arms exporters in the developing world. Without first-hand knowledge about its industrial infrastructure, it is not possible to judge the level of its technical and industrial capability. The video-tape of North Korean nuclear research activity made available by the IAEA seems to indicate not-very-modern, but competent technology, which may be going through a phase of technical difficulties in spent fuel typical of the Magnox reactor.[13] Until more detail becomes known, either through IAEA inspections or North–South mutual inspections, it is very difficult to estimate the possible impact of North Korean nuclear weapons in the future.

Japan's future defence
For a long time, Japan's basic defence posture was founded on the assumption that the Soviet Union was the potential enemy against which the US nuclear umbrella was deployed, but Japan's self-defense forces (SDFs) also contributed to the defence of the four main islands. This logic justified a number of budget items such as F-15 and next-generation FS-X fighters, modern heavy tanks to be deployed in Hokkaido and a small navy with a non-nuclear submarine fleet. The view was often expressed in Japan that the role of the ground SDF should be limited to law-and-order functions, including UN peace-keeping-type operations, that naval self-defence should be replaced by high-speed patrol boats with ship-to-ship missiles, and that the air force should have a more focused role. The 3,000-nautical mile sea lane was a plausible defence policy and emphasized cooperation with

the Seventh Fleet. It was never very clear what was considered the likely threat to this sea lane. A great deal will have to change in the US–former USSR relationship. What looked like a plausible defence plan is no longer valid, and even a reconstructed Russia will not pose the same military threat as did the former Soviet Union. China's intentions are less easy to define. The role of the US–Japan mutual security treaty is not as clear as it used to be. Japan wishes to retain US forces deployed and based in the country, which would be a politically important consideration. Paying the costs of stationing the US forces may no longer be sufficient, however, to ensure that they remain. If it does not, an expensive re-armament programme could ensue.

It is not easy to determine what kind of threat a unified Korea could pose to Japan's national security. With an alleged nuclear weapons programme in the North, it is not entirely inconceivable that a new and unified Korea might command ballistic missiles with ranges of 1,000 kilometres, armed with nuclear warheads. With the possibility of great confusion in China, it might be a prudent defence policy for Japan to start concentrating on anti-tactical ballistic missile (ATBM) defence against a small number of nuclear missiles homing in from the general direction of the Korean peninsula. Nuclear deterrence or offensive armaments are inconceivable options for Japan. Re-evaluation of the *Patriot* missile after the Gulf War seems to indicate that it would not be reliable for a country of Japan's size against re-entry speeds of more than nine times the speed of sound. It is possible that Japan may want to invest in cooperative arrangements with the global protection against limited strikes (GPALS) version of the Strategic Defense Initiative (SDI). The new direction of US–Japan security cooperation may be found in the preparation of technical and other options to defend against regional conflict involving a small number of medium-range nuclear missiles.

Another important component of such a defence/deterrence capability is a set of observation satellites providing early warning and tracking of incoming missiles, with information transmitted through relays to defence arrangements either on the ground or based in space. It is not clear whether the US would be willing to share such capabilities, as it has been treating satellite-related information as highly classified. With the resolution capabilities of the KH-12 and infra-red sensors, it would not be too difficult to observe operational modes and thus calculate the fuel burn-up of the Yongbyon reactor. If the United States knows the quality of North Korean plutonium, it has not shared that knowledge. Japan hopes to launch its own satellite through the development of the H-2 engine, which has experienced a series of failures and will be further delayed. Once Japan is in such a position, it may be feasible to establish an international organization for the joint launch and management of satellites, and for information-acquisition and data-processing purposes. It could serve as a multilateral arrangement to verify nuclear and other disarmament arrangements, it could serve as an early-warning system against preparations for attack and the actual launch of nuclear missiles and, if feasible, could also keep watch on environmental developments. So far, the verification of nuclear arms control and disarmament has been left in the hands of the two former superpowers, while the rest of the world listened to bilateral debates over possible violations of the unratified Threshold Test Ban Treaty of 1974 and the Strategic Arms Limitation Talks (SALT) II of 1979.

In the post-Cold War era, when the world is no longer bipolar, parties other than the two former superpowers should also be involved in satellite-based verification and related activities, which could help solve the problem of how to trigger IAEA special inspections (see above). That such an international satellite body should start with a rather restricted membership of those financially and technically capable and willing is a delicate and sensitive point. The 175-member (or more) UN General Assembly is not the ideal body to operate a technically oriented international organization.

One idea is to create an umbrella organization with enlarged membership. It would be possible to place the safeguards portion of the IAEA, the newly required organization to handle verifications under the Chemical Weapons Treaty, and the satellite organization under this international verification body. It seems that now is as good a time as any to start looking into such a possibility.[14]

Notes

[1] Coit Blacker and Gloria Duffy, *International Arms Control* (Stanford, CA: Stanford University Press, 1984) is a good reference work on the history of nuclear arms control negotiations.

[2] *Nuclear Fuel Cycle* (Washington DC: Energy Research and Development Agency, 1974) emphasized that a '[plutonium-fuelled] breeder program should be given highest priority, for commercial availability earlier than the present target date of 1993'.

[3] Technical aspects of the IAEA safeguards are discussed in Ryukichi Imai, 'Revision of International Atomic Energy Agency Safeguards, and Making IAEA Inspections More Effective', International Institute for Global Peace (IIGP) Policy Paper, nos. 59E and 90E.

[4] The W-85 warhead for the *Pershing*-II, as re-packaged into the B-61 'mod 10', is said to have some 1,800 different components. See 'Toward A Comprehensive Nuclear Warhead Test Ban', a report by the International Foundation, Singapore, January 1991.

[5] *Soviet Nuclear Fission, Control of the Nuclear Arsenal in a Disintegrating Soviet Union* (Cambridge, MA: Center for Science and International Affairs, J.F.K. School of Government, Harvard University, November 1991). Also, the testimony at the House Armed Services Committee (26 March 1992) given by General Burns, Head of the Safety, Security, and Dismantlement Delegation, State Department, Washington DC; and his testimony before the Senate Foreign Relations Committee, 29 July 1992.

[6] As discussed by Dr Edward J. Dowdy, Department of State, and others at the United Nations Disarmament Conference held in Hiroshima, Japan, 15–18 June 1992.

[7] The author was Japan's chief delegate to the Conference on Disarmament (Geneva) and the UN First Committee in 1983–86. He also served as chairman of

one of the preparatory committees, and the main subcommittee chairman at the 1985 NPT Review Conference.

[8] See, for example, Ryukichi Imai and Yasuhide Yamanouchi, 'International Transfer of Weapons and Related Technologies', IIGP Policy Paper, no. 79E, January 1992.

[9] The author is currently chairman of a subcommittee within the Japanese Ministry of International Trade and Industry (MITI) structure to review COCOM and other export control measures (including London Guideline, the MTCR and supercomputers) and to redefine Japanese policy regarding the future of COCOM.

[10] 'World Military Expenditures and Arms Transfers 1990', United States Arms Control and Disarmament Agency, November 1991.

[11] More discussion on the status of nuclear power and world energy may be found in Ryukichi Imai, 'Age of Plutonium, Nuclear Technology for Energy and Weapons Proliferation', a paper given at the 14th Oxford Energy Seminar (co-sponsored by OPEC, OAPEC and the Oxford Energy Institute) held at St Catherine's College, Oxford, on 8 September 1992. Ambassador Imai's 1991 lecture may be found in 'Nuclear Energy at the Crossroads', IIGP Policy Paper, no. 67E, August 1991.

[12] David Albright and Mark Hibbs, 'Iraq's Bomb: Blueprints and Aptfacts', and 'Iraq's Shop-till-you-drop Nuclear Program', *Bulletin of the Atomic Scientists*, January/February and April, 1992.

[13] The author was responsible at one time for the purchase of nuclear fuel and its post-irradiation disposal for the Tokai-1 power station, a 166-MWe gas–graphite reactor imported from the United Kingdom.

[14] Ryukichi Imai, 'Security and Development in the Asia–Pacific Region and Strengthening the United Nations and the Global Security Organization', IIGP Policy Paper, no. 61E, August 1991, and 'Expanding the Role of Verification in Arms Control', IIGP Policy Paper, no. 72E, February 1992.

The Consequences of Arms Proliferation in Asia: I

CHANCELLOR RO-MYUNG GONG

In the past few years, there have been profound changes in the international security order. The disintegration of the Soviet Union, with the collapse of communism both in the former Soviet Union and throughout eastern Europe, has brought the Cold War to an end, and out of the rubble has emerged a new US–Russian détente. This, in turn, has made it possible for many states, particularly those in Europe, to scale down significantly their military establishments. Adjusting to the new security environment, former arch-enemies in Europe are now working hand-in-hand to build a durable peace within the framework of the Conference on Security and Cooperation in Europe (CSCE).

These positive trends, however, have not yet extended to Asia, where Cold War sentiments linger and states continue to show deep-rooted mistrust and animosity towards their neighbours. Unsettled territorial disputes, military imbalance, regional rivalries, assertive military leaders and other sources of concern have kept countries on their guard, as have the perceived drawdown of the US military presence in the region and the need to prepare for the resulting uncertainties. Many countries believe that any diminution of the US commitment to regional stability could create a security vacuum that other major players would be either tempted or compelled to fill.

Although a few Asian states have begun to make modest defence cuts in this post-Cold War era, many others are engaged in the expansion of their defence capabilities. For instance, China is reported to have purchased 24 Sukhoi and 80 MiG-29 fighters, and has repeatedly increased its naval capabilities. Japan has also initiated a new five-year defence procurement plan that will increase defence spending in real terms by an average of 3% annually. In the Korean peninsula, North Korea is close to acquiring the capability to produce nuclear warheads. In addition, many of the Association of South-East Asian Nations (ASEAN) are currently establishing major arms acquisition programmes, involving the modernization and enhancement of air and maritime capabilities. In a word, there is a disturbing trend towards a regional arms build-up in Asia. As one observer puts it, Asia may soon become the most heavily armed region in the world as European arms reduction agreements are fully implemented.[1]

The military build-up in Asia
CURRENT TRENDS IN ARMS PROLIFERATION

According to available data, Asian countries have dominated the conventional arms import pattern over the last five years.[2] In 1989, developing countries in the Asia–Pacific region made up 59% of the imports of major arms by all developing states. Although this figure fell to 44% in 1990, in 1991 Asian countries accounted for 35% of all global imports of major weapons, more than any other region including Europe.

More precisely, of the leading importers of major conventional arms among countries of the developing world in 1987–91, seven Asia–Pacific states were among the top 15. Among all nations, three of the top five importers were in Asia – India, Japan and Afghanistan (in rank order). The other major importers in this region for the same period include the two Koreas, Pakistan, Thailand and Taiwan. Table 1 summarizes the recent trend in the arms build-up in Asia, and shows clearly the high rates of arms imports and military expenditures in the countries of the Asian region.

Table 1: Arms trade and military expenditure in the Asia–Pacific region, 1987–1991

	Arms imports (in millions of US$)	Arms imports as % of 1991 GNP	Military expenditure as % of 1989 GNP
India	17,562	6.0	3.1
Japan	9,750	0.3	1.0
Afghanistan	8,430	210.0	n.a.
Korea, North	4,631	10.0	20.0
Korea, South	3,552	1.0	4.3
Thailand	3,370	4.0	2.7
Australia	2,956	1.0	2.3
Pakistan	2,299	6.0	6.8
Taiwan	2,174	1.0	5.4
Indonesia	1,429	1.0	1.7
Singapore	1,276	4.0	5.1
China	797	0.2	3.7
Bangladesh	552	2.7	1.6
Cambodia	318	31.0	n.a.
Sri Lanka	274	3.0	3.2
Myanmar	268	1.0	3.7
Philippines	144	0.3	2.2
Laos	133	26.0	n.a.
New Zealand	106	0.2	2.2
Malaysia	105	0.2	2.9
Brunei	34	1.0	n.a.
Vietnam	6	0.0	n.a.

Source: Gerald Segal, 'Managing New Arms Races in the Asia–Pacific', *The Washington Quarterly*, no. 15, Summer 1992, p. 85.

Among the leading importers of significant weapons systems, the following developments deserve particular scrutiny for their effect on regional stability. First, as noted above, in 1991 Japan launched a new five-year defence procurement plan increasing defence spending in real terms by an average of 3% annually over the period. Despite the insistence that front-line equipment will be de-emphasized in the coming plan, a number of new systems are under consideration. These include Boeing E-3 Airborne Warning and Control Systems (AWACS), air-to-air refuelling tankers, additional *Aegis* systems and multiple-launch rocket systems (MLRS).[3] Moreover, Japan has recently agreed to allow its troops to take part in UN peacekeeping duties. This further adds to the perception that Japan is embarking on a long-term build-up of its regional military capability.

Second, China stands out in arms growth in the region because of its size and influence. In particular, China is expanding its navy and air force. It is improving the amphibious capabilities of its South Sea Fleet, constructing an air base in the Paracels and acquiring an air-to-air refuelling capability for its naval air force. Recently, the most significant development in China's arms expansion programme has been the purchase of 24 Su-27 combat aircraft from the former Soviet Union. China is also trying to purchase a sophisticated *Varyag*-class aircraft carrier, now under construction in a Ukrainian shipyard.[4]

Third, India is significantly expanding its navy. It plans to acquire another aircraft carrier, more surface combatants, more Dornier Do-288 long-range maritime patrol aircraft, and a modern conventional and nuclear-powered submarine fleet. It is also gradually developing its naval and air facilities on the Andaman and Nicobar Islands – which are only 80 nautical miles from the north coast of Sumatra.[5]

Fourth, in the South-east Asian region, all ASEAN countries – with the exception of the Philippines – are transforming their naval capabilities from essentially surface warfare-oriented patrol boat/coastal forces to navies with greater range and a broader spectrum of capabilities. For example, they are now all equipped with *Harpoon* and/or *Exocet* anti-ship missiles. They are also acquiring maritime surveillance and modern fighter aircraft, which can be used in maritime attack roles.[6]

Beyond these developments, proliferation of advanced military technologies – including weapons of mass destruction (nuclear, chemical or biological) – and delivery capabilities (in particular, ballistic missiles) are an additional concern. In the region, China and Russia are acknowledged nuclear powers. Since the early 1990s, however, five more Asian countries – India, Pakistan, North Korea, Iraq and Iran – are assumed to be developing nuclear weapons. Among them India is believed already to possess nuclear explosive devices and may be on the verge of open nuclear deployment. This spread of nuclear weapons, without a doubt, heightens regional politico-military instability.

The proliferation and development of ballistic missiles is of even greater concern. Currently, 16 Asian nations possess ballistic missiles,

12 of them capable of producing the systems domestically.[7] Imports and exports of such ballistic missiles within the region are also of great concern. For instance, a series of North Korean shipments of *Scud* missiles to Iran, Syria and other Middle Eastern countries clearly denotes a massive military build-up in the region. Even as the great powers have launched an ambitious scheme, such as the Missile Technology Control Regime (MTCR), to control them, the quest for modern armaments among the Asian countries continues unabated.

THE MOTIVES AND RATIONALE BEHIND THE MILITARY BUILD-UP

What are the motives and rationale behind the arms build-up in the region? In theory, military build-ups and arms races are manifestations of insecurity, but they may also result from the ability to pay for new weapons.[8] However, the motives and rationale behind the military build-up in Asia are complex and vary according to country.

In recent years, several factors have facilitated arms proliferation in the region. First, many states are preparing for potential instabilities which may arise when the US reduces its military presence. The larger regional powers wish to consolidate their positions and increase their influence, while the smaller countries hope to play a more active role in the region.[9]

Second, the widespread need to replace ageing equipment is coupled with the economic resources to do so – and with modern high-tech weaponry. In recent decades, the most important changes in Asian countries have taken place in their economies. Asian economies have grown rapidly, and this economic growth has provided many countries with the power to purchase advanced high-tech weapons. In particular, the large trade surpluses enjoyed by China, Taiwan, ASEAN and other countries are helping to fuel the dangerous arms race in the region.

Third, historical anxieties and territorial disputes continue to weigh in the balance. There are numerous areas of current or potential conflict in East and South Asia, such as Kashmir, the Irian Jaya–Papua New Guinea border, the Spratly and Paracel Islands in the South China Sea and disputed island and continental shelf claims in the Gulf of Thailand. Faced with these areas of potential instability, many states need to upgrade their outdated weapons and keep pace with military deployments in neighbouring countries.

Fourth, domestic pressure from an influential military establishment cannot be underestimated as a factor in increasing military expenditure. For example, in China the defence budgets have grown by an average of more than 12% in the past few years, despite an increasingly peaceful security environment and the normalization of ties with former enemies, such as the Soviet Union, India and Vietnam. This increase in military resources has been due largely to the role played by the People's Liberation Army (PLA) in suppressing the pro-democracy demonstrations in Beijing in June 1989. In Thailand, the military's influence in the policy-making process is also one of the main reasons it has acquired sophisticated weapons systems.

In addition to these factors, the market-oriented arms sales policy of some arms suppliers – most notably the former Soviet Union – is contributing to a dangerous arms proliferation in the region. Attempting to convert the military-industrial complex into an export industry, Russia, Ukraine, Byelarus and other former Soviet republics make no secret of their desire to create out of Asian countries with huge trade surpluses – particularly China – a lucrative market for their excess weapons. For instance, in May 1992, President Yeltsin told defence plant managers that Russia would try to market $5 billion-worth of arms yearly to China. Arms sales are now making ex-rivals Moscow and Beijing comfortable bedfellows, and this is helping to fuel dangerous arms proliferation in Asia.[10]

Strategic implications of arms proliferation
The most dangerous aspect of the recent military build-up in Asia is its spiralling effect. In some senses, the current military expansion in the region is close to a traditional action–reaction cycle of arms races. For instance, China's naval build-up is keeping pace with the Japanese. Some analysts argue that China's desire for its own aircraft carriers stems from concerns that Japan will one day acquire such a capability. In reaction, Japan is proceeding with the production of weapons using its own technology, and watching China's naval expansion closely. The Chinese arms build-up is also having a great impact on ASEAN and Taiwan. The strengthening of their naval capabilities has largely to do with China's expanding military presence in the South China Sea, including the Spratly and Paracel Islands.

Continued arms proliferation in Asia is likely to have extensive international consequences. It is already having a definite effect on relations between states in the region, influenced by military and strategic considerations, and will almost certainly significantly accelerate regional tensions and suspicions. Ultimately, the escalation of arms proliferation could lead to open military hostilities and potentially to the use of nuclear weapons.

Asia is a region of chronic tension, embracing several areas of potential instability, and the military growth in the region will no doubt increase the frequency and lethality of conflicts. In particular, the spread of ballistic missiles, with their technical characteristics including the speed with which they can reach targets, their relative invulnerability to defences, their adaptability for delivering warheads of mass destruction and their special utility for pre-emptive military operations, will pose serious security dilemmas that will be difficult to eliminate.

In addition to increasing regional tensions, the continued trend towards arms proliferation in Asia will have the most adverse economic consequences. This means that current extensive military expenditure may fall because of its negative economic effects in an area of regional economic strength and dynamism. Over recent decades, the Asian economies have had larger periods of more rapid growth than any other economies in world history. As a result, Asia has become the main source of dynamism in international trade, and the largest source of surplus savings for international investment. However, the current trend towards extensive military spending in the Asian countries could erode their underlying economic capabilities and the full potential of the region.[11]

Finally, Asia's arms proliferation could have a great impact on the alignment of powers in the region. That is, it could alter existing alliances. For instance, the US–Japan security relationship has been widely viewed as crucial to regional stability, having often been described as a vital linchpin of peace and security throughout Asia and the Pacific. Keeping a check on Soviet aspirations in the area, it has also contributed to reassuring the region about Japanese intentions. However, the logic underpinning the US–Japan alliance remains essentially rooted in the Cold War era, linked to the military threat posed by the Soviet Union and its client states. In the post-Cold War era, with the Japanese defence budgets increasing and its military capabilities growing, there are concerns about the potential erosion of US–Japanese security relations. Memories of Japanese imperialism linger on in the region; and although many Japanese officials pledge that Japan will never become a military power that would threaten any other nation, it will become so if it pursues an independent military role outside the parameters of the US–Japan security pact. Without the glue of a common threat, and with incentives for Japan to go its own way, US–Japanese security relations could be undermined. No doubt the potential erosion of these relations would have a negative impact on the security relations among the Republic of Korea, the US and Japan.

Controlling arms proliferation
The negative impact of arms proliferation in Asia calls for its control and ultimate elimination. This can be justified by considerations other than the security and economic priorities discussed above. Arms proliferation in Asia could extend from the regional to the global level, feeding worldwide tensions and conflicts. With the spread of longer-range ballistic missiles in particular, local or regional military conflicts could have wider international consequences. Armed with nuclear, chemical or even advanced conventional munitions, these systems could expand the scope of conflict well beyond the combatant states.[12]

At this moment, the discussion about how to control the arms build-up in Asia is in an embryonic stage. It is only in recent years that a number of diplomatic initiatives for organizing Asian regional security have been created to remove the risks of arms races or even conflicts. Since the early 1990s, for instance, several states in the region have proposed the establishment of a Conference on Security and Cooperation in Asia (CSCA) modelled on the lines of the CSCE.

Because of the power asymmetries in the Asia–Pacific region and existing diverse threat perceptions, any discussion of multilateral security cooperation has been regarded as premature. However, the idea of a CSCA is gathering support, as regional conflicts are expected to intensify and become more complex. Many states in the region now acknowledge the need for a multilateral approach to security in the Asia–Pacific. There is also a re-evaluation of the CSCA concept in one form or another by the regional states.[13] The necessity for regional security consultations can no longer be neglected, and it is time to study ways to develop a security dialogue for the Asia–Pacific as a means of enhancing confidence, dissipating possible tensions and reducing the arms build-up.[14] In the absence of any multilateral framework for international cooperation at the subregional or regional level, there are real risks of an arms race and even hostilities in Asia.

No less vital for reducing the risks of arms proliferation in the region is the need to strengthen existing arrangements and institutions and the bilateral negotiations between the parties directly concerned. Currently, various efforts to stop the proliferation of nuclear weapons are being employed, especially in the light of the loopholes that are becoming apparent as the Iraqi nuclear weapons programme is being dismantled. More resources should be made available to the International Atomic Energy Agency (IAEA) in conjunction with an enhanced safeguards commitment and, at the same time, nuclear export controls should be tightened.

Other efforts – for example, the development of an effective MTCR – might be useful in the region. The MTCR currently coordinates national export restrictions on the transfer of missiles and the technology for missiles capable of carrying a 500-kg pay-load over a range of 300 kilometres. As the number of participants has increased in recent years, far more attention needs to be given to signing up new members in Asia.[15] This arrangement is still far from effective in stopping determined national desires to acquire long-range ballistic missiles, but it is a good example of a multilateral effort that is making improvements.

Bilateral negotiations between the parties directly concerned should also be emphasized. A number of direct negotiations are already being observed in North-east and South-east Asia. For instance, the reconciliation and non-aggression agreement and the denuclearization declaration between North and South Korea have been adopted. In addition, there are continuing negotiations between China and Russia to establish, in effect, a demilitarized zone between the two countries and to institute European-style confidence- and security-building measures (CSBMs), such as advanced notice of manoeuvres and exchanges of military information. At the subregional level, these bilateral negotiations will make the North-east Asian area a safer and more peaceful place. In these cases, however, written pledges alone are unlikely to bring peace. Sincere and effective implementation of the negotiated agreements is the key to genuine peace and security.

Conclusions
In this post-Cold War era, the positive trends in the international security environment have not yet extended to Asia. On the contrary,

the region is being engaged in a nuclear and conventional arms build-up, influenced by perceived uncertainty and insecurity, outstanding territorial disputes, regional rivalries and other sources of concern. If this current trend continues, it will have extensive international consequences, increasing the frequency and lethality of conflicts. North-east Asia, in particular, including the Korean peninsula, presents the greatest risk if proliferation escalates.

The potential negative impact of arms proliferation in the region calls for its control and ultimate elimination. In order to reduce the risks of the arms race or even conflicts, the importance of regional security cooperation cannot be overemphasized. It is time to study ways to develop security dialogue for the Asia–Pacific region.

To emphasize the importance of multilateral dialogue and cooperation in security matters is not necessarily to deny the role of the existing arrangements and the bilateral negotiations between the parties directly concerned. Certainly it will not be a substitute for close bilateral relations where they already exist. Rather, they are complementary to each other in halting the dangerous arms build-up in Asia.

Notes

[1] Douglas M. Johnston, 'Anticipating Instability in the Asia–Pacific Region', *The Washington Quarterly*, no. 15, Summer 1992, p. 103.

[2] *The SIPRI Yearbook, 1992* (Oxford: Oxford University Press, 1992), and *The Military Balance, 1991–1992* (London: Brassey's (UK) for the IISS, 1992).

[3] US Congress, Office of Technology Assessment, *Global Arms Trade* (Washington DC: US Government Printing Office, 1991), p. 111.

[4] *The Washington Post*, 14 July 1992.

[5] This information is based upon Desmond Ball, *Building Blocks for Regional Security: An Australian Perspective on Confidence and Security Building Measures (CSBMs) in the Asia/Pacific Region*, Canberra Papers on Strategy and Defence, no. 83 (Canberra: Australian National University, 1991), p. 10.

[6] *Ibid.*, p. 11.

[7] Janne E. Nolan, *Trappings of Power: Ballistic Missiles in the Third World* (Washington DC: The Brookings Institution, 1991), p. 8.

[8] Gerald Segal, 'Managing New Arms Races in the Asia–Pacific', *The Washington Quarterly*, no. 15, Summer 1992, p. 83.

[9] Johnston, *op. cit.* in note 1, p. 105.

[10] Jim Hoagland, 'Russian Arms to China: Japan Steps In', *The Washington Post*, 14 July 1992.

[11] *Study on the Economic and Social Consequences of the Arms Race and Military Expenditures* (New York: United Nations, 1989), p. 61.

[12] Nolan, *op. cit.* in note 7, p. 9.

[13] The ASEAN nations agreed to a security consultative body; and Japan proposed upgrading the ASEAN Post-Ministerial Conference (PMC) to include more dialogue on political and security matters.

[14] At the ASEAN PMC meeting in July 1992, the Foreign Minister of the Republic of Korea, Lee Sang-ock, stressed the need to develop regional consultation on common security in Asia and the Pacific where security has long been maintained largely by a 'web of bilateral arrangements led by the US'. See *The Korea Herald*, 25 July 1992, p. 2.

[15] As of May 1992, the total number of MTCR members was 18. One of them is an Asian country – Japan. Recently China suggested that it was studying the regime.

The Consequences of Arms Proliferation in Asia: II

DR GERALD SEGAL

It can be argued that the risks of nuclear and conventional arms proliferation are greater in Asia than anywhere else.[1] With the dismantling of Iraq's nuclear programme under way and progress being made on de-nuclearizing all of the former Soviet republics except Russia, the nuclear proliferation spotlight is beginning to turn to Asia. While India and Pakistan are coy about the extent of their nuclear capability, there is growing concern that a nuclear overlay has been added to their intense rivalry, a rivalry that has already led to war. Most worrying of all, North Korea's attempts to acquire a nuclear capability have been identified by American officials as the most important security threat in East Asia.

The proliferation of conventional weapons in Asia is equally apparent. It accounts for a greater proportion of the conventional weapons trade than anywhere else. Defence budgets in the region are growing, and many of the newly acquired weapons are of such lethality and range that they complicate calculations of threat and risk, even if current political disputes do not yet seem especially intense. What is perhaps most worrying is that the wealth of many East Asian states is making possible the acquisition of the most modern technology. If these states should find that in the pursuit of national security they undermine international security, they will be wreaking havoc in the most rapidly growing part of the global market economy. War, or even arms races, in East Asia would be far more damaging to the global economy than conflict in the Middle East.

Of course, the proliferation of weapons *per se* is not the primary problem. A more complete assessment of the risks depends on a more rounded sense of the sources of the danger.[2] There is no simple way to assess the main risks or costs of proliferation, if only because of the range of possible criteria for concern. Therefore the roots of risk must first be explored, before looking at the consequences of proliferation.

The sources of tension

A cursory glance at Asia reveals a complex pattern of hot spots. Unlike Europe, there are virtually no places in the region where the fires of conflict are actually raging, in sharp contrast even to the mid-1980s when the IISS last held a conference in the area.[3] But in many places around Asia there are embers of conflict that would require little fanning before they flared up. Korea, South-east Asia, India–Pakistan and Central Asia are all obvious examples of simmering tensions. There are other, less immediate, but in some senses more worrying, risks including potential rivalry between China and Japan. A brief survey of these issues must include the following.

RAPID AND UNEVEN RATES OF DEVELOPMENT
As much as rapid development can be applauded, it is important to recognize the risks involved. Development, whether in China, the newly industrializing countries (NICs) or even Japan, tends to exacerbate social tensions as the benefits of growth are unevenly distributed. Although growth in the NICs has been remarkably equitable, expectations are raised in different ways for different segments of the population. Some in Taiwan believe independence is becoming a more realistic option and thus tensions rise with China. Growth in China has been concentrated in coastal regions, leading to tension in centre–province relations and raising concerns about tendencies towards division. China has been divided in the twentieth century, not to mention in preceding centuries, and global economic interdependence may well help pull it apart. Rapid development, when it outpaces political reform, runs the risk of destabilizing the social system and even the basis for further growth. Managing democracy and development are obviously of key importance in South Korea, Taiwan and Singapore. Even Hong Kong is affected by such issues, and some might say that the Japanese political system will have to modernize if it is to sustain economic growth in the next century.

LEADERSHIP INSTABILITY
One of the worrying aspects of the relative absence of entrenched pluralist democracies in Asia is that the vagaries of leadership politics play such an important part in managing international security. The succession in China is perhaps the most obvious uncertainty, for on its outcome depends such vital matters as whether China will accept interdependence and eschew nationalist irredentism. The succession in North Korea is a critical factor in managing both Korean reunification and perhaps even a nuclear weapons crisis. In Central Asia, few people expect the current leadership to be much more than a transition from communist rule. Deep fears surround the successor leadership, such as the rise of Islamic or ethnic fundamentalism, or opportunities for neighbouring powers to exploit instability.

PROBLEMS OF POVERTY
For all its wealth, East Asia, and certainly Asia as a whole, contains some of the poorest states in the world. Needless to say, the likes of Laos and Bangladesh cannot afford to spend money on weapons. But some, like Vietnam and Myanmar, have spent far too much on hardware, although Vietnam at least seems to be mending its ways. Afghanistan is also spending less, but then it has virtually ceased to exist as an effectively unified state. India and Pakistan rank high on the list

of arms purchasers, although they are among the poorest places on earth. China is in roughly the same poverty league, but has increased its defence spending for several years running. The poor but new states of Central Asia have barely begun to work out their own defence arrangements, but although they cannot really afford arms races, this may not stop them from feeding the deep insecurities that divide them from each other and from their neighbours outside the former Soviet Union. Those states who can so ill-afford to spend on military equipment are also those who most often demand aid from the developed economies while denying them the right to express a view on how that money should be spent. The link between aid and unwelcome military policies will become an obvious bargaining tool for those who wish to stop conflict in Asia affecting the prosperity of both the region and the wider world.

ETHNIC AND RELIGIOUS DISPUTES
Not all of Asia suffers from ethnic tensions, but where the problems exist, they make recent events in the Balkans seem almost insignificant. Murderous clashes between the Central Asians took place even before the Soviet Union collapsed. Only a cursory appreciation of what happened in Afghanistan is necessary to understand how unpleasant conflicts in this region can get. India and Pakistan have already demonstrated their dubious credentials in such conflict, both within their own states and between the two of them. Myanmar's treatment of its minorities has spilled over into tensions with both Bangladesh and Thailand. As these and other conflicts have demonstrated, ethnic tensions are often accompanied by the migration of refugees which further complicates a difficult conflict.

    Ethnic patchworks exist in South-east Asia, but at least the tensions seem more controlled. Essentially Chinese, Singapore has a wary peace with Malaysia as do the Malays with their Chinese minority. Indonesia wages war on the people it controls in East Timor, but this is not seen as anything more than the usual brutishness of one regime to its subject people. Chinese behaviour in Tibet, Inner Mongolia or Xinjiang is no different, although the latter case has increasing implications for international relations between neighbours. But it is conceivable that at least some of these tensions, for example between Malaysia and Singapore, could fuel arms races and even conflicts.[4] Fortunately, in most of the rest of East Asia there is a remarkable congruence between ethnic groups and state frontiers.

TERRITORIAL DISPUTES
Where ethnic disputes cross frontiers, territorial disputes also appear – none more viciously than in Kashmir. The frontiers in Central Asia are new as international boundaries, but already obviously ludicrous and therefore likely to figure in future conflict. Older disputes, such as that

between China and Russia, are well on their way to being settled. Younger disputes, such as that between Japan and Russia, are still a bone of contention. Japan, China and Taiwan dispute the Senkaku islands, but have agreed to put the issue to one side for the moment. Would that the same could be said for disputes in the South China Sea where China, Vietnam, Taiwan, Malaysia and the Philippines claim all or part of the islands and the surrounding water and resources. As this area sits astride some of the most important waterways through which trade to East Asia flows, the interests of North-east Asians are also drawn in. Given the complexity of the conflict and the importance of the region, this must rank as one of the most important disputes in Asia. In February and July 1992, China seized a few more islets from Vietnam, as if to remind the world of the dangers in the region.

DIVIDED STATES
Some of the other more dangerous conflicts occur where once united countries have been divided. The Korean conflict is the most obvious case, and equally the most obvious candidate for crisis. As it is located in North-east Asia and surrounded by some of the world's most powerful countries, the outcome is the most vital for international security.

The fate of China is only somewhat less worrying. Despite growing economic interconnections, it is far from clear that Taiwan and China are growing more politically united. Indeed, it can be argued that as the tendencies towards division in China develop, even the integration of Hong Kong into China may help pull the country apart. As Taiwan acquires an increasingly sophisticated arsenal, and China develops its longer-range military hardware, a major crisis in the Taiwan Strait cannot be ruled out. It is the height of 'econophoria' to suggest that economic interdependence will only lead to peace, and will not instead help feed conflict.

ENVIRONMENTAL ISSUES
This is a much under-researched problem, although some work on South Asia has shown that environmental issues are only a small part of much more complex relations.[5] But there is some evidence in the more developed parts of East Asia that environmental matters are of increasing concern.[6] Given the prevailing winds, Chinese and Korean pollution drifts over Japan. Japanese firms, anxious to get rid of their most polluting industries, export such production to their subsidiaries in South-east Asia. Malaysian misuse of tropical forests puts it at the forefront of international campaigns. When China builds a nuclear power station close to Hong Kong, the issue clouds already difficult relations. While none of these disputes have so far involved the threat of force, they certainly have added to tensions in the region, and may do so even more as the richer states of East Asia can afford to be concerned about environmental matters.

A NEW BALANCE OF POWER

This last category of risks is perhaps what most people at an IISS conference would discuss, but it is only a problem if the previous seven problems cannot be handled. A change in the balance of power or the creation of a power vacuum is not necessarily a problem. If the retreat of what was Soviet power and the drawing down of American power were to take place in a region where existing multilateral security and political networks could cope with most major disputes, then the risk might be contained. The perceived need to retain a major American presence to 'hold the ring' or 'balance the wheel' is only necessary because there is so much uncertainty about the reaction of other states in the region.[7]

Much anxiety surrounds the behaviour of China and Japan – the two most probable fillers of a vacuum. Both countries are likely to be rivals and both play on essentially different fields, with China preferring military power and Japan having obvious economic strengths. It is in this context that possible arms races in East Asia become worrying, and most neighbours would like to see such a race stopped before it gets out of hand.[8] But with little tradition of multilateralism in the region, states tend to seek national means of enhancing security, thereby feeding uncertainties in neighbouring countries and damaging international security. At a minimum, uncertainty about the American presence is a major part of the drive for arms acquisition and, to some extent, American firms are happy to fill the orders. Should the United States feel that it can or must scale down its forces in a major way, it seems inevitable that regional arms races will develop. In the absence of a multilateral security framework, there is little reason to be optimistic that 'econophoria' will keep everyone calm.

At first glance Asia does not seem as obviously dangerous as Europe. More people in Europe (if one includes the Caucasus) are dying in conflict these days, a development unprecedented since the 1930s. But first impressions are misleading. Conflicts in Europe are peripheral to the richest Europeans and it is striking how well multilateralism has worked in Europe to keep the major powers out of direct conflict. The absence of multilateralism in Asia is therefore deeply worrying.[9] To an important extent, Europeans may also be reacting quicker to the end of the Cold War, largely because it affected Europe more deeply than it did Asia. But Asians too will have to face the consequences of the new world disorder.

The consequences of proliferation vary a great deal and the problems that result cannot be tackled at the same time. A number of issues stand out as the most pressing. First, the consequences of nuclear proliferation in North-east Asia are deeply worrying. Not only would this make conflict in that vital region more likely, and perhaps make Korean reunification less likely, but as proliferation spread to Japan, the worldwide non-proliferation regime would be shattered.

Second, the main risks of conventional weapons proliferation are increased lethality and the ability to project power. These risks are most acute when political conflicts are less constrained, and therefore it is the conjunction of these factors that should cause the greatest concern. Possible conflict between China and Japan is both a medium-range and a longer-range concern. Tension in the South China Sea is far more acute, and perhaps so is conflict between China and Taiwan, or in the India–Pakistan nexus. Conflict in East Asia would be particularly worrying for any damage to the local economy would be bound to affect the global market economy. These disputes are assessed in detail elsewhere in these conference papers, but suffice it to say that any attempt to deal with the risks of such consequences of proliferation will have to focus on a mixture of technological, economic and political factors.

Coping with the consequences
It has become 'trendy' to toy with the idea of arms control in Asia, and because even the most formerly sceptical (especially in the United States) have climbed aboard this bandwagon, there has been an abundance of proposals on the best way to proceed.[10] In the areas of tension identified as being of the utmost importance, all the conflicts have their essential roots in the domestic politics of the states concerned, and yet all have a role for outside states. Because the risks of proliferation in Asia are multifaceted, so the control of these risks requires a complex approach. Arms-control edifices that are not built with these diverse blocks will be unsteady.

UNILATERAL EFFORTS
One of the most striking aspects of arms control in Asia is that the most far-reaching progress has been made by states acting unilaterally. Only after unilateral steps are taken do they sometimes seek codification in formal arms control. Unilateral reductions by the Soviet Union and China in the 1980s were crucial to their subsequent more formal détente. Vietnam followed a similar path when, for essentially domestic reasons, it cut the size of its armed forces and thereby made détente with China and the Association of South-East Asian Nations (ASEAN) states more possible. Even India, with its budget-crunch, can be said to have joined in the mutually reinforcing pattern of unilateral arms reductions.

These unilateral efforts have played their part in reducing Sino-Russian rivalry in Korea, and therefore in making possible an inter-Korean solution. The prospects for North-east Asian arms control depends on détente between Russia and China. Both these countries, and especially China, can exert influence on North Korea to abandon its nuclear weapons programme, and both have done so. Also, the fact that Russia and China have put such a priority on economic reform and a peaceful international environment has added to the pressure for reform in Pyongyang. Both Russia and China know that if they fail to manage the Korean problem, their own positions in the region will suffer grievous harm.

BILATERAL EFFORTS
The only significant formal arms control in Asia has been bilateral, and efforts at this level continue to be vital to building security. The dialogue between the two Koreas had spluttered into life at various stages, but in the 1990s the engines have begun to roar. None of the accords reached so far can prevent the outbreak of war, but they are helping to build confidence and develop a habit of dialogue. Current discussions are over matters that could create greater transparency on nuclear weapons issues – the most sensitive issue in the region. But no accord reached between the two Koreas would be sufficient in and of itself to reassure the international community. There are plenty of suspicions about the implications of a reunified Korea for North-east Asian states, so that a bilateral accord could only be part of a complete security structure. Under some circumstances, a purely inter-Korean deal without the involvement of the broader international community might even increase tension in the region.

Bilateral efforts at building confidence elsewhere in Asia are less complex. When India and Pakistan reached an accord (ratified in 1991) on not attacking each other's nuclear installations, there were few suspicions from either country's neighbours. Yet part of the reason why India feels it cannot accept restrictions on its nuclear capability on a bilateral basis with Pakistan is a real worry about China. With uncertainty about nuclear issues in Central Asia, both India and Pakistan have reason to fear that bilateral accords would be insufficiently subtle to deal with the new risks in their region.

Bilateral arms control had also been agreed between the then Soviet Union and China. As already suggested, this process had important domestic sources and in turn had an important effect on related issues such as Korea. But the accord on confidence-building measures was also significant in that it helped codify détente in what was once the most dangerous zone in Asia. Few details are available about the verification procedures in this agreement, but there is so much less concern about the risk of war between these two East Asian giants partly because such an accord could be reached.

Less formal arrangements have been made between China and Vietnam. Nevertheless, political détente between these two states is of obvious benefit for regional security, both in terms of helping reach a settlement on Cambodia, and for wider South-east Asian issues. Although there was some concern that this was part of a 'red solution' that might pose a threat to non-communist states in the region, it is now recognized that Sino-Vietnamese détente is uneasy.[11] It certainly does little to deal with the risks of conflict in the South China Sea. Indeed, a formal non-aggression pact between China and Vietnam that included the South China Sea might even be interpreted by some South-east

Asians as increasing the risk of their own conflict with China. Despite the Sino-Vietnamese détente, South-east Asian states are spending large amounts on conventional arms in part because they perceive no real reduction in tension in the region. Once again, bilateralism in arms control is not enough.

SUBREGIONAL EFFORTS
In Asia's three main subregions (North-east Asia, South-east Asia and South Asia), there has been progress in two areas, but nothing in the most important subregion for global security – North-east Asia. South Asia has the South Asian Association for Regional Cooperation (SAARC), although its prohibition on discussing domestic issues means that a security dialogue is virtually impossible in an area where so many issues begin with domestic roots. Yet an institutional framework for discussing problems is useful, even if they must be muttered about in corridors. Of course, it makes little sense for the Maldives to be present when India and Pakistan discuss Kashmir, but there is some gain in easing the fears of smaller states that the main protagonists might be carving up the region to suit themselves. Of course, given the complexity of regional politics, it is not surprising that SAARC has no major formal achievements to its name.

South-east Asia has long had ASEAN, although the organization does not yet include the states of Indochina and until recently had no formal role in security matters. The decision at the 1992 summit to include formal discussions of security is little more than a formalization of corridor diplomacy and recognition of new needs in the uncertain post-Cold War world. It can be argued that ASEAN was always essentially a political and economic institution born out of shared security concerns over Indochina. Yet formal attempts at building security cooperation always took place outside ASEAN, whether in the failed context of the South-East Asia Treaty Organisation (SEATO) or the less ambitious but still successful Five Power Defence Arrangements (FPDA). The FPDA links Malaysia and Singapore with New Zealand, Australia and Britain and reinforces the argument that South-east Asia has failed to arrange its own security dialogue. In times of uncertainty and arms races after the Cold War, this gap becomes a larger problem. And yet the main risk in the region – the South China Sea – cannot be resolved simply in an ASEAN context. Dialogue must also include China, Taiwan, Vietnam and perhaps even Japan.

North-east Asia is the focus of interest for four great powers, and conflict in the area could be more devastating to the global economy than anywhere else apart from western Europe. Therefore it is all the more peculiar that no subregional institution in any field has emerged. Current attention lingers on the Canadian initiative in shaping a security dialogue in the North Pacific, but this is a tentative process bedevilled by American and Japanese suspicions about the need to move from bilateralism to multilateralism. The two Korean states also resent attempts to turn what they see as their private tiff into a version of the

European 'Two Plus Four' arrangement for a divided Germany. The
Canadian initiative has also tried to cover other issues such as the
environment, migration and human rights, but in the end its primary
contribution will be in helping provide for more transparency in security matters and helping create a habit of dialogue. It is important that
the United States is now discussing Korean issues with Japan and
South Korea – the first time such multilateralism has been accepted,
even among notional allies. Clearly there is a long way to go before a
far-reaching multilateral security scheme can be developed for North-
east Asia, but there are increasing signs that the security lacunae are
being addressed. Of course, such matters as nuclear proliferation in
Korea cannot be handled simply, either on a bilateral or a subregional
level.

REGIONAL EFFORTS
Some of the most long-standing and least realistic proposals for arms
control in Asia have included the creation of a region-wide arrangement. The Australians have been much maligned for suggesting a
Conference on Security and Cooperation in Asia (CSCA), and not
surprisingly the idea lies buried in academic journals. But as the Asia–
Pacific Economic Cooperative (APEC) process builds, there is renewed talk of some sort of Asia-wide forum dealing with security.
Current ideas include turning the ASEAN Post-Ministerial Conference
(PMC) into a more formal meeting of foreign ministers from the
region, but the dismally ineffective response at the July 1992 ASEAN
PMC to the Chinese seizure of yet another islet in the Spratlys, sug-
gests this group is unlikely to become effective. Some suggest that
even APEC might be given a role in the security sphere.[12]

After so many years of neglecting multilateral relations it would be
churlish to suggest that there is no role for a CSCA or an ASEAN
PMC. But as the basic functions of fostering transparency and a habit
of dialogue are developed at the subregional level, it becomes increasingly incumbent on supporters of a CSCA to demonstrate what discussions at this level would add to the building blocks of security. The
South China Sea dispute is perhaps the only issue that might justify a
CSCA approach, but by convening a meeting of only the core state (as
Indonesia did), it has been shown that the likes of Mongolia and South
Korea (let alone the South Asians) need not be involved. Other topics
are best handled subregionally, for example Korea or India–Pakistan
tensions, or else at the global level, for example controlling the arms
trade. In sum, it might be sensible to pay far less attention to regional
groups while concentrating on building security on lower and higher
levels.

GLOBAL EFFORTS
Events in Asia have had major consequences for the rest of the world,
whether they be wars in Korea, Vietnam or South Asia, or the transfor-

mation of the global market economy by the emergence of dynamic economies in East Asia. Therefore it should not be surprising that there is a close relationship between Asian security and changes in the global system. Indeed, it can be argued that any solution to Asia's problems of nuclear and conventional weapons proliferation must include major efforts at the global level.

The risks of proliferation in North-east Asia and South Asia are part of a global process. The acuteness of the concern over North Korea's nuclear weapons programme is closely related to the failures of the old system to identify the extent of the risks in the Iraqi case. To an important extent the North Korean case has become a test of the ability of both the International Atomic Energy Agency (IAEA) and the international community to cope with the post-Cold War world. A solution to the North Korean problem requires work at the bilateral and subregional levels, but the most reliable efforts will be undertaken by the IAEA and perhaps even by a United Nations Security Council-mandated effort to impose intrusive inspections and possibly even sanctions. Failure to limit proliferation in North Korea is a failure for the international community and therefore of interest to the wider world. It is not enough for the Koreans to argue that this is a matter for themselves to sort out.

Similarly, the risks of proliferation in Central and South Asia are part of the global agenda. International efforts to reduce the proliferation in Central Asia that accompanied the break-up of the Soviet Union have already achieved many of their objectives. But further south, India and Pakistan continue to delay efforts to deal with the risks of proliferation. Although China has now signed the Nuclear Non-Proliferation Treaty (NPT), India declines to do so and is therefore out of step with the international community. Such action, although not as obviously dangerous as in the North Korean case, also deserves to be treated at the global level. Whether aid to India is restricted until it complies with international norms, or whether aid to China is limited until it ceases large nuclear weapons tests, is more a debate about tactics than about the need to treat the risks of proliferation as a matter of global concern.

As regards the spread of conventional weapons, the international system is far less advanced in its methods. The Missile Technology Control Regime (MTCR) is not a formal treaty and is only beginning to gain some weight. The United Nations Arms Register is not yet in operation, and there is serious doubt about whether states will comply with its basic requests for a modicum of transparency. Efforts by the five permanent members of the Security Council (Perm 5) to control the export of conventional arms to the Middle East suggest that there is not yet a successful model that might be transferred to Asia.

What is clear is that the problem of the proliferation of conventional arms cannot be properly handled at just a regional or subregional level. Given the presence of powers with global reach (America or Russia), and the presence of local powers with a multiplicity of interests (China, India, Japan), it is impossible to calculate a reasonably stable balance of arms. The Conventional Armed Forces in Europe (CFE) accords did not restrict forces in the eastern section of Eurasia, although the more optimistic might suggest that a northern hemisphere accord (from Vladivostok, via Vancouver, to Vladivostok) is not beyond the realm of possibility. But given the difficult in dealing with only the western portion of the Northern hemisphere in the post-Cold War world, such an effort seems unlikely.

Even if it proves impossible to get anything more than agreements on greater transparency in the transfer of conventional arms, it is clear that attention must be paid to the risks of unconstrained arms races in Asia. It is not always that the states of the region cannot afford new weapons (although for some this is the case), or that defence spending will rise as a percentage of the gross national product. With fast-growing and wealthy states, parts of Asia can afford an arms race in an economic sense. But the real risk to their prosperity is from the ensuing damage to the balance of power. The growing range and lethality of weapons in a region with deeply engrained historical disputes must make most observers worry about how to keep the region stable in the future. Destruction or even reduction in the prosperity of East Asia will damage the prosperity of all those integrated in the global market economy.

A la carte security
For those fond of finding differences between Europe and Asia, few contrasts are as striking as the fact that, while Europe now has more wars than Asia, Asia has a far bigger problem with nuclear and conventional weapons proliferation. In essence, both Europeans and Asians are adapting to the post-Cold War world, although they do so in different ways. Europeans will note that for all their new wars, they at least have some multilateralism that helps them cope. Asians who fear for their ability to meet the challenge of the post-Cold War world note that they have virtually no multilateralism on which to build security. While the challenge for Europe is to make its multilateralism work in new conditions, the Asians are engaged in the far more basic task of building a habit of multilateral dialogue.

Multilateralism is far too often seen as a set menu, where either the entire meal is taken or there is no place at the table. The reality of much of European multilateralism has been far more *à la carte* dining, even in the European Community (EC). Asia too would benefit from a more *à la carte* approach, if only because it would make the kind of bespoke security (to change the image)[13] that the individual states feel they need easier. Dealing with the risks of proliferation in North-east Asia requires unilateral steps, as well as bilateral efforts between the two Koreas or between interested great powers and a Korean state. The region would also benefit from action directed specifically at the North-east Asian or even North Pacific subregion. Efforts at the global level are certainly needed, especially when it comes to the risk of nuclear proliferation. Similar mixes of security from different levels can be applied to tension in South-east Asia or South Asia. Detailed discussion of these problems are undertaken elsewhere in this conference, but suffice it to say that the *à la carte* approach to security means that local states cannot argue that their disputes are only for themselves to resolve. In an interdependent world such a line of argument is untenable, especially when it comes to nuclear weapons. Neither should states outside the region think that security in Asia is only for the Asians to decide. The logic of interdependence is both economic and military, for it is increasingly clear that economic interdependence is not enough to ensure peace and stability.

Notes

1 Gerald Segal, 'Managing New Arms Races in Asia–Pacific', *The Washington Quarterly*, no. 15, Summer 1992; Andrew Mack, 'The Nuclear Issue on the Korean Peninsula', *Foreign Policy*, no. 83, Summer 1991; Andrew Mack and Desmond Ball, 'The Military Buildup in Asia–Pacific', *The Pacific Review*, vol. 5, no. 3, 1992, pp. 197–208; David Shaw, 'Defence Spending in Southeast Asia', *Military Technology*, no. 2, 1992.

2 For a less worried assessment of the region, see Gary Klintworth, 'Asia–Pacific: More Security, Less Uncertainty, New Opportunities', *The Pacific Review*, vol. 5, no. 3, 1992, pp. 221–32.

3 Robert O'Neill, *East Asia, the West and International Security* (London: Macmillan, 1987).

4 Tim Huxley, 'Singapore and Malaysia: A Precarious Balance', *The Pacific Review*, vol. 4, no. 3, 1991, pp. 204–13.

5 Shaukat Hassan, *Environmental Issues and Security in South Asia*, Adelphi Papers, no. 262 (London: Brassey's (UK) for the IISS, Autumn 1991).

6 Min Young Lee, 'Resource Supplies and Dependence in the North Pacific', and Vclav Smil, 'Potential Environmental Conflicts Involving Countries of the North Pacific', papers published by the North Pacific Cooperative Security Dialogue Research Programme, University of York, Toronto, 1992.

7 James Winnefeld, Jonathan Pollack, Kevin Lewis, Lynn Pullen, John Schrader and Michael Swaine, *A New Strategy and Fewer Forces* (Santa Monica, CA: The Rand Corporation, 1992).

8 Harlan Jencks, 'China's Defense Buildup', and Taeho Kim, 'China's Military Buildup in a Changing Climate in Northeast Asia', papers prepared for the Conference on PLA Affairs of the Chinese Council of Advanced Policy Studies, Taipei, Taiwan, June 1992.

9 The argument is developed in Gerald Segal, 'North–East Asia: Common Security or A La Carte', *International Affairs*, vol. 67, no. 4, October 1991.

10 Patrick Cronin, 'Pacific Rim Security: Beyond Bilateralism?', *The Pacific Review*, vol. 5, no. 3, 1992, pp. 209–20.

11 Michael Williams, *Vietnam at the Crossroads* (London: Pinter for the Royal Institute of International Affairs, 1992).

12 Geoffrey Wiseman, 'Common Security in the Asia–Pacific Region', *The Pacific Review*, vol. 5, no. 1, 1992, pp. 42–59, and, in general, *The Pacific Review*, no. 4, 1991.

13 John Chipman, 'The Future of Strategic Studies', *Survival*, vol. 34, no. 1, Spring 1992.

The Security and Economy of a Reforming India

PROFESSOR RAJU THOMAS

India faces a variety of challenges to its security, economy and democracy in the 1990s. Changes in the global, regional and internal security environments, increasing levels of ethnic conflict and armed insurgencies, and concurrent Indian efforts to switch from a heavily socialist-oriented economy to a free-market capitalist system, have placed considerable stress on the Indian democratic system and process. The advent of successive minority central governments in New Delhi since 1989 has made the task of coping with the dramatic changes even more difficult.

The success or failure of the Indian government in responding to these changes and crises of the 1990s will have a significant impact on the stability or instability of the South Asian region and beyond. The perseverance with democracy in India, for instance, has had a contagious effect in the rest of South Asia. Since 1988, Pakistan, Bangladesh and Nepal have joined India and Sri Lanka as democratic states. On the other hand, political instability, economic chaos or even the disintegration of India could have adverse spill-over effects in the rest of South Asia. Another Indo-Pakistani war over Kashmir may not only trigger more Hindu–Muslim communal violence in India, but would set the economies of both countries back several years. And an Indian decision to embark on a formal nuclear weapons programme could undermine the nuclear non-proliferation regime in North-east and West Asia, and compel the former republics of the Soviet Union in Europe and Central Asia not to give up their nuclear weapons.

Redefining India's security and economic policy must take into account two significant developments in the international and domestic arenas. At the international level, there has been an increasing concentration of economic and military power in the West so that the old security and economic choice between East and West is no longer available to the developing countries. The ability of the West to enforce military solutions to regional conflict issues was displayed during the 1991 Gulf War when the Iraqi annexation of Kuwait was quashed by UN-sponsored military action. The disintegration of the Soviet Union eliminated the 'Soviet card' which developing countries had exploited to advance their regional claims and military objectives during the Cold War. With the economies of the former communist countries of Europe now in shambles, the ability of the developing world to seek foreign economic assistance and industrial investments is also now confined to the Western world.

At the domestic level, the increasing dependence of national defence programmes on the import of high-tech weapons tends to deplete the availability of scarce foreign exchange reserves for development programmes. The opportunity costs of defence and development have become more stark and critical in recent years. Consequently, the need to resolve regional conflicts peacefully has become more urgent to enable poorer countries such as India to concentrate on economic development.

The dilemmas of security, development and democracy

Underlying the various issues that India faces in the 1990s are questions of economic priorities and political means – between allocations of resources to defence and development, and between the level of democratic or authoritarian means that should be adopted to achieve security and economic objectives. More security through an arms build-up may mean less economic development. Less development may lead to more problems of internal security. Widespread economic deprivation and frustration may provoke violent protest movements among the lower-middle class and the impoverished masses, or may lead to inter-ethnic and inter-caste strife over territories and scarce resources. More internal violence may lead to less democracy and perhaps even an end to democracy. On the other hand, less democracy (or even no democracy) may mean more development as wasteful public-sector undertakings are dismantled, trade unions are curtailed and national economic and social disciplinary regulations are introduced. More development may mean more resources being available for the Indian arms build-up thereby leading to an arms race and heightening political tensions in the region.

Some of these dilemmas may be seen in the Indian experience over the last three decades. First, the years of neglect of Indian defences that led to the crushing defeat in the 1962 Sino-Indian War produced the realization that development without sufficient defence was dangerous to the well-being of the state. Thereafter, there was debate in India about how much should be allocated to defence without putting the development programme at risk. Opponents of the Indian defence build-up argued that more allocations to the defence programme might result in even more having to be allocated later as adversaries began to match or exceed India's military capability. Thus, more defence may prove to be counterproductive for both defence and development. For example, the anti-bomb lobby in India has argued that an Indian decision to embark on a nuclear weapons programme would inevitably result in a Pakistani nuclear build-up and make the Chinese nuclear threat even more menacing than before. India would become caught up in an irreversible three-way nuclear arms race. The net result would be less Indian security at a much higher price.

Second, there is some sentiment in India – especially in government circles – that the democratic process may have to be curtailed or suspended in the interests of both security and faster rates of economic development. In the interests of security, for instance, the Sino-Indian War of 1962 led to the passage of the Defence of India Act. Similarly, the crisis leading up to the Indo-Pakistani War of 1971 produced the Maintenance of Internal Security Act. Both Acts restricted individual freedoms by giving the Indian government the right to preventive detention without trial, and recourse to other measures that bypassed parliamentary procedures. Such measures are permissible under various emergency clauses of the Indian constitution, especially Article 352. Thereafter, growing internal unrest and violence led to a series of Acts and Amendments. These included the National Security Act of 1980 and the Terrorist and Disruptive Activities (Prevention) Act of 1987 that gave the government special powers to deal with insurgencies in Punjab, Kashmir and Assam.

In the interests of faster rates of economic growth, the question arises of whether a democracy is the right political system for a poor country with a multitude of economic problems that need to be addressed urgently. In India, democracy has sometimes meant the pursuit of economic policies that carry short-run appeal to largely illiterate electoral masses rather than policies that are likely to produce long-term economic benefits. No doubt, the illiterate Indian voter has often displayed shrewd 'political literacy' in the sense of understanding which politicians are more likely to meet basic local social and economic needs. However, the average Indian voter has little understanding of more sophisticated macroeconomic policies. Thus, political manifestoes advocating centralized socialism may win elections, but may not achieve rapid economic growth. This was the case with the Congress Party's economic policies in India for decades. On the other hand, manifestoes that advocate private-sector capitalism have had difficulty winning elections in India. The demise of the Swantatra Party in 1980, a party which had been created as the secular private-sector alternative to the Congress Party in 1959, is indicative of the unpopularity of the capitalist ideology in India. Even Prime Ministers Indira Gandhi and Rajiv Gandhi had to talk socialism for public consumption purposes while implementing more private-sector capitalist policies in the 1980s. Again, violent and disruptive trade union movements in a democracy can also shake industrial confidence and thwart economic progress in the public and private industrial sectors. The massive trade union movement in India is capable of paralysing the economy for days, and therefore has considerable bargaining power with the government.

While the West may have achieved its economic prosperity through the democratic process, doubts have been expressed as to whether developing nations can 'afford the luxury of a democracy'. Industrialization and prosperity in the democracies of Britain, France and the United States, for instance, were achieved through steady economic growth over several decades, going back even to various industrial breakthroughs in the late nineteenth century. On the other hand, spectacular and sustained GNP growth rates of 8–12% in South Korea, Taiwan and Singapore, and more recently in China, Thailand and Indonesia, were all achieved under authoritarian regimes. Sustained high rates of economic growth over a period of about two decades would seem to require political, economic and social discipline, national behaviour that may be more easily enforced in dictatorships. For example, China has the advantage over India in enforcing strict population control policies crucial for faster rates of economic growth.

Only the post-war democracy of Japan, and more recently that of Malayasia, have matched the successful economic performances of the other Asian countries functioning under authoritarian systems. However, in spite of the formal existence of a Western-style democracy in Japan, the Japanese people appear to function in a regimented and disciplined manner almost as though they were living under an authoritarian system. This kind of Japanese self-discipline would seem unthinkable in the Indian democracy. The Indian (perhaps 'Hindu') way of thinking and working cannot be regimented and disciplined in the Japanese way. India is much too individualistic and unshackled a country, allowing for a multitude of expression and actions.

Third, underlying many of the problems of ethnic separatist insurgencies and domestic violence in India are economic grievances. Thus, demands for an independent Assam or Telengana state by mainly Hindu Assamese or Telugu-speaking peoples come from a sense of economic exploitation or deprivation. The underlying causes of conflicts in Kashmir and Punjab are not entirely (or even primarily) Hindu–Muslim or Hindu–Sikh religious antagonism. The Kashmiri demand for independence arose from the feeling that the central government, while subsidizing the state, did not invest sufficiently, and that the senior levels of state government employment had largely gone to Kashmiri Hindu Pandits rather than to the Kashmiri Muslims. Many Sikh nationalists feel that the prosperity of Punjab is being unfairly exploited through higher progressive federal taxation which is then redistributed to less efficient states such as Bihar.

In general, rapidly rising expectations among the growing middle class, as high as 15–20% of the population (about 150–180 million people in 1992), portend deep and widespread dissatisfaction that must be met through rapid and equitable rates of economic growth. Access to communal television and radio facilities in the villages is making the impoverished Indian masses aware of their relative state of economic deprivation. Unless their expectations are met quickly, India could be faced with explosive revolutionary conditions by the turn of the century.

Faced with these dilemmas, the Congress government of Prime Minister P.V. Narasimha Rao has sought to address the manifold external threats perceived by redefining India's relations with the United States, Russia and China. India's policies towards its neighbours and the neighbouring regions, especially Central Asia, are also being reformulated. The government has embarked on fresh efforts to resolve the various destabilizing domestic conflict conditions especially in Kashmir, Punjab and Assam. And a concerted attempt is being made to move towards a private-sector free-market capitalist economy within the established Indian parliamentary system of democracy. However, during Rao's first year in office (1991–92), India's search for new ties with the great powers remained unsettled; its internal security problems seemed to remain the same or get worse; its efforts to privatize and 'de-bureaucratize' ran into hurdles; the economy turned sluggish amidst the worldwide recession; and there was some concern over whether the Indian parliamentary system is capable of handling these monumental challenges of the 1990s with the urgency needed.

The new security environment
Problems of external and internal security faced by India appear increasingly intertwined in the 1990s. Wars may occur on the subcontinent because of internal armed insurgencies in Kashmir, Punjab and Sindh that may spill across the international borders of India and Pakistan. The continuing dangers of conventional and nuclear wars in South Asia that may undermine the territorial integrity and survival of the state, have been overshadowed by the dangers of domestic armed insurgencies and terrorist strategies engaged in by various dissident ethnic groups.[1] Combatting the internal 'enemy' has proved to be more prolonged, costly and often unsuccessful than combatting the external enemy. The problem has been aggravated by the conduct of proxy wars across national frontiers. Pakistan has provided training and material assistance to Kashmiri and Sikh insurgents in India. India assisted the Tamil separatists in Sri Lanka before 1990 by providing sanctuaries in the Indian state of Tamil Nadu. Pakistanis now allege that India is assisting the Sindhi separatists in Pakistan, especially the Al-Zulfikar Organization.

In the past, India perceived threats primarily from Pakistan and China, and much of its defence preparations were directed at these two states. More broadly, there were general perceived threats from the growth of nuclear weapons among the nuclear powers, especially China, and the increasing presence of great-power navies in the Indian Ocean during the Cold War. The Pakistani, Chinese, nuclear and naval threats have substantially changed since the beginning of this decade. Relations with China have greatly improved, and the nuclear threat is perceived to stem mainly from Pakistan rather than from China. The commencement of Indo-American military cooperation, especially between their navies, and the decreasing presence of the French and Russian navies, have lowered Indian perceptions of a naval threat by the great powers. However, this has not dampened India's belief that its navy will have a major role to play in the defence of India and the maintenance of regional stability between the Horn of Africa and the Strait of Malacca.

The most important change has been the emergence of a new but as yet vague 'Islamic' threat – an indeterminate complex mix of 'external', 'internal' and 'transnational' threats. The main external component of the Islamic threat remains the Pakistani military capabilities which may be augmented by arms transfers from other Muslim states in West Asia. To this may be added the internal 'Islamic' threat which stems from India's increasing inability to manage Hindu–Muslim communal conflict within the country. The spread of vociferous Islamic fundamentalist politics from various parts of the Muslim world to India's 120 million Muslims constitutes a rising transnational threat contributing to the potential instability of the Indian state.

Responses to external developments
The immediate post-Cold War period generated confusion and uncertainty within the Indian foreign and defence policy-making bureaucracies. This confusion may be seen in various Indian efforts to forge military ties with the US, negotiate a new Indo-Russian Treaty to replace the old Indo-Soviet treaty, formulate a new policy towards the Muslim world, and at the same time salvage some use for the Non-Aligned Movement (NAM). In particular, two events in 1991 had a profound effect on Indian security policy-makers. First, the easy destruction of Iraq's extensive Soviet weapons arsenal by the allied forces in the Gulf War raised doubts about the effectiveness of the same or similar Soviet military equipment in the Indian military. The spectacular performance of Western high-tech precision weapons against Iraq increased the concern of the Indian military about their own likely performance against adversaries who may have access to such Western weapons.

Second, the disintegration of the Soviet Union removed the central pillar around which India had formulated its diplomacy and defence strategy. India had been dependent on the Soviet veto in the Security Council in past debates on Kashmir and during wars with Pakistan. Various quasi-military clauses embodied in the Indo-Soviet Treaty of Peace and Friendship signed in August 1971 provided India with some assurance that Chinese or American military intervention in the subcontinent against its security interests would be deterred if war broke out between India and Pakistan. The renewal of the Treaty in August 1991, just before the disintegration of the Soviet Union, displayed a monumental failure of Indian intelligence causing temporary disarray in India's foreign policy. Negotiations to draw up a new Indo-Russian Treaty along the same lines have not yet produced results.

Indian efforts to forge closer ties with the United States had begun with the signing of a Memorandum of Understanding on technology transfers in 1986. These ties were further advanced with the visit of an American defence delegation to India in December 1990. Following the Gulf War and the collapse of the Soviet Union, India's efforts to upgrade its military ties with the United States was accelerated. These ties soon began to take on the shape of a near-alliance relationship, well beyond the ties that existed earlier between India and the Soviet Union, or even between the US and Pakistan. Throughout 1991, there were several exchange visits by military delegations from both sides. The first Indo-American naval exercise took place in May 1992, and a second was scheduled for September 1992.

The early exuberance in India for closer Indo-American ties began to fade by mid-1992 as old disputes continued to resurface and new ones began to emerge. Past Indo-American friction over the Special 301 provisions of the 1988 Omnibus Trade and Competitiveness Act of the US Congress (known popularly as 'Super 301'), and India's unwillingness to accept international patent rights in the area of pharmaceuticals, continued to restrain the growth of Indo-American ties. Another point of friction arose in 1992 over the Indian Space Research Organization's (ISRO) decision to purchase a cyrogenic rocket engine from Russia's space agency, Glavkosmos.[2] The United States sought to bar the sale on the grounds that it violated the rules relating to the sale of propellants and propulsion systems of the Missile Technology Control Regime (MTCR). Russia claimed that it was not party to these rules and, in any case, as both India and Russia declared, the cyrogenic engine had no direct military use. Despite Indian and Russian protestations, the US introduced a two-year ban on all trade and technology transfers to ISRO and Glavkosmos as a penalty for the proposed sale. With the US Congress threatening to withhold a $4.35 billion aid package to Russia, Moscow showed signs of backing out of the deal.

Creeping disillusionment arising from a sense of manipulation by the West in both India and Russia has begun to bring the two countries closer together again. Mutual Indo-Russian security concerns are also being discovered in the potential rise of unstable Islamic governments in the Central Asian republics. Although there may be as yet no major strategic considerations for establishing Indo-Russian military ties, Moscow still remains a relatively cheap source of military hardware for India, provided New Delhi can find the necessary hard currency that Russia now demands. However, such Russian weapons for hard currency are not available to India alone. Pakistan is also negotiating the purchase of MiG-29s from Russia, and of other ex-Soviet military equipment from eastern Europe.

Whereas efforts to promote Indo-American cooperation have run into obstacles, Sino-Indian relations appear to be returning to the good old days of 'Hindi-Chini Bhai-Bhai' ('Indians and Chinese are brothers') that prevailed briefly in the 1950s. The new ties were heralded by the visit of Premier Li Peng to New Delhi in December 1991, and then cemented by the visit of President R. Venkataraman to China in May 1992. These two exchange visits produced brave declarations to oppose 'international oligarchies' and the determination to resist being 'bullied by others', references clearly directed at the concentration of economic and military power in the West. The growing warmth in Sino-Indian relations is also being accompanied by a certain distancing between China and Pakistan. Compared to India's reiteration of its position in the 1950s that Tibet was a part of China, the Chinese made no reference to Kashmir during the December 1991 talks in New Delhi. This would suggest that China still upholds its old pro-Pakistani position that Kashmir is disputed territory. Nevertheless, Beijing must surely be concerned that independence for Kashmir could spell trouble for Tibet and perhaps even for its Turkish Muslim-inhabited province of Xinjiang.

India's proximate and main foreign policy concern in the 1990s is the potential spread of transnational Islamic fundamentalism from the north-west. Transnational Islamic beliefs and methods are evident in the insurgency in Kashmir. Pro-independence and pro-Pakistani Kashmiri militants have absorbed the Islamic fundamentalist ideology from Iran, the techniques and methods of the *intifada* movement from the West Bank, and the strategy of the liberation struggle of the Afghan *mujaheddin* during their war against the Marxist regimes of Kabul. Developments just beyond the subcontinent have made the 'Muslim factor' in India's foreign policy more significant than in earlier decades. The secular Najibullah government that India had supported has been replaced by an Islamic government in Kabul, thus adding to the two other Islamic states of Pakistan and Iran. There are concerns in India that Islamic governments will eventually come to power in the two poorer Central Asian republics of Tajikistan and Uzbekistan as the ex-communist leaders of these countries start to fall or fade away.

Meanwhile, Pakistan is in search of economic and military ties with the Muslim countries of West and Central Asia. Islamabad has already sponsored membership in the Economic Cooperation Organization of all the five Central Asian republics and Azerbaijan, thus expanding its economic partnership with the other original members, Iran and Turkey. The purpose of these moves is to create an Islamic political counterweight to what Pakistanis perceive as Hindu India, and to provide the country with strategic strength in case of another war with India. India has sought to counter these moves by encouraging the establishment of secular democracies in the new Muslim republics. Every head of state of the Central Asian republics visited India within six months of their independence. Joint communiqués with Kazakhstan and Kyrgyzstan included statements on the importance of secularism for regional stability.

There are, of course, limitations to Pakistani efforts to forge a larger Islamic or Muslim confederation. There are major differences in population sizes and socio-economic levels. The 1991 per capita incomes in the Central Asian republics varied from $3,240 in Kazakhstan to $1,460 in Tajikistan compared to $360 per capita in Pakistan, and the literacy rates are almost 100% in all the republics compared to 30% in Pakistan.[3] Pakistan's population is 115 million compared to 60 million in the Central Asian states. Most of the Central Asian states have also expressed a preference for the Turkish democratic secular model to that of Pakistan, Iran or Saudi Arabia.[4]

The possibility of a larger Pakistani-conceived Islamic bloc of nations counterbalancing India may appear unlikely at present, but it is sufficient to worry Indian policy-makers. India is conscious of the fact that transnational Islamic movements could have deleterious consequences for India's domestic stability, and for the subcontinent. The rise of radical Islamic fundamentalism in Afghanistan and Pakistan, in addition to that which already exists in Iran, could spread to India's 120 million Muslims aggravating current Hindu–Muslim tensions and internal conflict.

The nuclear and naval threats to India appear to have partially receded with the restoration of the *entente cordiale* between India and China, and with the end of superpower naval rivalry in the Indian Ocean. But there has been little change in India's nuclear and naval policies. India and Pakistan are currently on the brink of nuclear weapons capabilities, or perhaps already possess them. Depending on whether the two states are 'on the brink' or are 'in possession', international and regional demands continue for the creation of a 'nuclear-free zone' or a 'nuclear-safe zone' in South Asia. Even if India and Pakistan have made the transition to nuclear weapons capabilities, the situation may still be reversed since both sides are unlikely to possess more than two or three 'bombs-in-the-basement' at present. Indeed, those analysts in India and Pakistan who claim that it is too late to establish a 'nuclear-free zone' and argue instead that they must concentrate on establishing a 'nuclear-safe zone', are usually those who also prefer to see the nuclearization of South Asia. A nuclear South Asia would presumably prevent even conventional wars, though not the kind of intermittent low-intensity war in the Siachen Glacier, or the prolonged proxy wars in Kashmir, Punjab and Sindh. However, some degree of stability that may be obtained in the region through nuclearization would be considerably offset by the global destabilization brought about by the predicted end of the nuclear non-proliferation regime.

There is, however, one fallacious argument in the West about India's nuclear plans that must be dispelled. The opportunity costs of India's nuclear and missile programmes are not as substantial as is sometimes imagined. India assesses these proposed nuclear military programmes as an 'incremental cost' over its ongoing civilian nuclear energy and space programmes. It is a matter of diverting some plutonium and rocket parts to the military programmes. In fact, the economic burden of a nuclear weapons and missile programme is more likely to arise from the retaliatory economic sanctions that will be imposed by the West rather than from research, development and production. The growth in Indian naval capabilities in the 1980s has slowed down along with the general decline in Indian military capabilities. The decline in defence spending in the early 1990s has been brought about by the domestic economic and budgetary crises and the foreign-exchange costs of a continuing Indian military build-up. Arguments for naval expansion in India still rest largely on the need to defend India's long coastline, its 200-mile maritime zone, and to protect Indian shipping in the Arabian Sea and Bay of Bengal. However, like nuclear weapons power, India also views naval power as an international status symbol. Nuclear weapons, along with India's growing intermediate-range ballistic missile capabilities and naval power, provide it with an extended military reach that goes well beyond subcontinental defence. The ability to exercise such 'power projection' would ostensibly give India an 'Asian', if not 'great-power', status, a status it was denied throughout the Cold War.

Responses to internal security crises
The main threat that India faces in the 1990s lies within its borders. These growing internal threats to India may be distinguished as the more 'general' and the more 'specific' types. The general kind may be seen in the scattered Hindu–Muslim religion-based violence, and the often widespread violence among Indian workers during calls for national *bandhs* (the cessation of all business activities). Both occurrences tend to make the central and regional governments appear unstable, weak and ineffective. If governments are perceived to be weak and unstable, the danger of general disintegration may then arise as various states and regions may not find it worthwhile to remain part of the Indian Union.

However, it is specific ethnic separatist movements in the various states and regions that pose the greater threat of Indian disintegration. The 'domino'-type of state disintegration that occurred in the Soviet Union and Yugoslavia could well be replicated in India. At one time, India faced demands for independence in what are now the tribal states of Nagaland, Mizoram and Meghalaya in the north-east corner of India. The populations of these regions are less than two million, and they possess little economic value. Their struggle for independence dissipated after eventually being granted statehood within the Indian Union. But with independence struggles taking place in the major states of Punjab, Kashmir and Assam – all at the same time – the government of India now faces a crisis of far greater proportions than during the first three-and-a-half decades since independence. All three states carry strategic, political and economic significance.

The location of Kashmir and Punjab along the Pakistani borders, together with Pakistan's long-standing claim to Kashmir, make these two states particularly vulnerable to external threats. The demand by most of the four million Muslims in the Vale of Kashmir for independence or accession to Pakistan threatens the future of the remaining 115 million Muslims. Indian Muslims would have to live through another partition of India on the Muslim question. Moreover, Kashmiri independence may be followed by the independence of other Indian states similar to the chain of copy-cat declarations of independence made by all the republics of the former Soviet Union and Yugoslavia.

Whether such fears are exaggerated or not, India appears determined to resist the Kashmiri independence struggle indefinitely. On the other hand, the hardcore Kashmiri insurgents seem determined to continue with their *'jihad* for *jihad*'s sake' whatever the outcome of the struggle. The objectives of most Kashmiris remain unclear. They have swung from support for the pro-independence Jammu and Kashmir Liberation Front (JKLF) militants to the pro-Pakistani *Hizb-ul-Mujahideen* (HUM) and the *Ikhwan-ul-Muslimeen* (IUM) militants, and back to the pro-independence JKLF insurgents again. These swings suggest that India may be able marginally to pacify the Kashmiris in the long run with economic concessions and an eventual return to the ballot box. However, bringing Kashmir back to the pre-1987 election situation looks to be a hopeless task in the short run.

The Punjab crisis involves separatist violence by a key ethnic minority group, the Sikhs, who have constituted the backbone of the Indian armed forces. Punjab is also the bread-basket of India, a state that has become all the more crucial after the greater part of the old Punjab was incorporated into Pakistan in 1947. A solution to the Punjab problem is as yet nowhere in sight. The elections in Punjab in February 1992 were expected to bring about some semblance of a return to democracy and normality. Out of conviction for their cause, or fear of the militants who threatened to kill those who participated in the elections, nearly all the factions of the Sikh *Akali Dal* party boycotted the elections. The exception was the Kabul faction of Captain Arminder Singh (the former Maharaja of Patiala). As a consequence, voter turnout was less than 30% (mainly Hindu), and the Congress Party was returned to power.[5] Unfortunately, the Congress Party Chief Minister, Beant Singh, has been unable to curtail the continuing violence.

The government of Narasimha Rao has now agreed to implement the 1985 Harchand Singh Longowal–Rajiv Gandhi pact in its entirety. The pact had been held up until now because of objections from Haryana, a state separated from the Hindu majority areas of Indian Punjab in 1966 in order to give Sikhs a majority in Punjab. This pact provided the transfer of water resources and land from Haryana to Punjab, and agreed to make the city of Chandigarh the sole capital of Punjab, instead of both states as was the situation after the creation of Haryana. If the Longowal–Gandhi pact had been implemented back in

1986, it may have settled the crisis and brought most of the Sikh moderates back into the Indian mainstream. But efforts by the Narasimha government to implement the 1985 pact in 1992 may perhaps be too little and too late.

As with Kashmir and Punjab, Assam is strategically located. It lies beyond the narrow corridor between Bangladesh and Bhutan. The loss of Assam could unravel all of India. Initially, an independent Assam may open up a Pandora's box of new independent states in the region. The entire north-east sector of India beyond Bangladesh – Assam, Manipur, Tripura, Nagaland, Mizoram and Meghalaya – would be lost. Sikkim would be difficult to retain within India. Assam would also be the first Hindu-majority state to gain independence and could trigger similar secessions in the other Hindu majority states and districts of Tamil Nadu, Karnataka, Telengana (Andhra Pradesh) and elsewhere.

A solution to the Assam problem is being attempted through military force. Four Indian Army divisions and over 200 paramilitary companies have been deployed since 1990 to bring the separatist United Liberation Front of Assam (ULFA) to sue for peace. However, a military solution, if achieved, will last only if a political solution is also found that redresses the grievances of the Assamese. After all, the ability of the ULFA to conduct their operations over the last decade was made possible through the shelter and support given by sympathetic Assamese villagers and townspeople.

A purely military offensive against the Kashmiri and Sikh insurgents is even less likely to succeed since the insurgencies in these two states can be fuelled indefinitely from across the borders by Pakistan. There are limits to the ability of the Indian security forces to plug the holes across the border from where arms and insurgents move freely. At best, the cross-border movements of the insurgents may be restricted, but they cannot be contained entirely. Unlike Assam, there are also too many groups and leaders involved in the separatist struggles in Kashmir and Punjab: in Kashmir they include the JKLF, HUM and IUM; in Punjab they include the Khalistan Liberation Force, the Khalistan Commandoes, the Bhindranwale Tigers of Khalistan and the *Babbar Khalsa*. Successful negotiations with one group will not necessarily end the terrorism and insurgency engaged in by others. And unless a settlement can also be reached with Pakistan on Kashmir, the proxy war will continue from across the border in both states.

Finally, the rise of the Hindu fundamentalist parties and organizations such as the Bharatiya Janata Party (BJP), the *Vishwa Hindu Parishad* (VHP), the *Rashtriya Swayamsevak Sangh* (RSS) and the *Shiv Sena* has increased the level of tensions between Hindus and Muslims. India may not have an external security doctrine, but there is a clear-cut internal security 'attitude', if not doctrine, namely that no part of its territory will be allowed to secede. Such a policy is akin to the Brezhnev doctrine of the 1960s and 1970s with respect to the bordering communist states of the Soviet Union: that force would be used if any of these states sought to break away from the Soviet bloc.

India has resorted to military suppression (including alleged violations of human rights) on the one hand, as well as political concessions and efforts to conduct democratic elections on the other, in order to cling tenaciously to all of its territories.

The success of this Indian doctrine is quite surprising with respect to Kashmir and Punjab because these two important non-Hindu majority states have had powerful overseas supporters in the British and European parliaments, and in the US Congress. Many notable overseas politicians have recommended independence and recognition for these two states. Indeed, Kashmiri Muslim and Punjabi Sikh separatists expected the same treatment as that accorded to the ex-republics of the Soviet Union and Yugoslavia. In particular, Kashmiris were sure that independence was in sight since the state was internationally recognized as disputed territory whose status had yet to be settled. Their expectations of independence were not fulfilled and the prospects have continued to recede. India has simply made violent demands for independence internally and stonewalled diplomatic pressures externally.

As with his other policies dealing with foreign relations and economic problems, Prime Minister Narasimha Rao has taken a quiet, low-key approach to resolving the internal threat problems of India. Rao's different style from that of Congress prime ministers of the 'Nehru dynasty' has not produced any political success as yet in Kashmir, Punjab or Assam. Perhaps the problems lie more deeply in the nature of the federal structure and process of the Indian political system. The Indian constitution provided too much central government authority at the outset for such a diverse and multi-ethnic state as India. Subsequently, as internal strife multiplied and magnified, a further concentration of power was obtained by the central government in New Delhi through a series of acts and amendments in order to deal with terrorist activities. These new acts and amendments appear to provide methods only of coping with internal security problems on an *ad hoc* basis rather than of finding permanent solutions.

The new development agenda

The transition from emphasis on public-sector capitalism to private-sector capitalism was begun rather slowly from about the mid-1970s under Congress Prime Minister Indira Gandhi. The tempo of economic change was increased under Prime Minister Rajiv Gandhi after the election of 1984 when he won 79% of the seats in the lower house of the Indian parliament. However, it was only after the minority Congress government of P.V. Narasimha Rao took office in June 1991 that sweeping economic liberalization and reform were introduced into the Indian economy.

There is relatively little dispute among the mainstream members of the three major political parties – Congress, the BJP and *Janata Dal* – that India must move away from socialism. But there are differences of opinion among these parties on how much reform there should be, and how fast these reforms should take place. There is also opposition to economic liberalization or the type of reform that should take place among factions within the three major parties. Apart from members of the Communist Party Marxist (CPM), a minority of left-wing members within the Congress Party and *Janata Dal* are opposed to abandoning India's primarily socialist system. Even within the ranks of the Hindu-religious right-wing BJP, which had always included (or was viewed sympathetically by) prominent members of the business community, there are differences over the nature of economic reform that should be adopted. Hindu nationalist leaders such as L.K. Advani, B.R. Malkani and A.B. Vajpayee are enthusiastic advocates of an open free-market system that would provide incentives to both Indian capitalists and foreign investors. However, other BJP leaders, such as Murli Manohar Joshi who are more Hindu 'fundamentalist' in their ideology, advocate a reform movement that would emphasize *swadeshi* or indigenous capitalism.[6] Underlying this pro-Hindu belief in promoting 'made in Bharat' capitalism, is the fear that the influx of Western or Westernized multinational enterprises would corrupt Hindu values and the Indian way of life.

Unlike some of the ex-communist countries of Europe which are attempting to convert to a capitalist system, in India, private initiative, entrepreneurial skills and market-oriented capitalism are inherent in sections of Indian society, and especially in the Hindu caste hierarchy. Indian capitalists were kept on a leash through 40 years of Indian socialism, but continued to practise successfully under the most difficult political and economic handicaps. In July 1992, the *Financial Times* of London described the Indian business community as the most 'buccaneer capitalists' to be found anywhere in the world. Again, unlike the ex-communist countries of Europe, all the institutions and processes of capitalism are already in place and functioning in India, so that what is required is merely the unshackling of an existing system. On the other hand, it must also be remembered that there are various sections of Indian society, especially in the Hindu caste hierarchy, which regard the business community and private greed as distasteful and immoral. After all, it was Jawaharlal Nehru, the high-caste Brahmin, who insisted on implementing Stalinist-type socialist economic plans in India, albeit within a democracy that conformed to his high moral and political ideals. These two conflicting intellectual, social and political forces in India will continue to out-manoeuvre each other as they have done in the past. However, for the time being the capitalist experiment has been given a chance, and the success of this experiment could change irrevocably the direction of Indian economic policy in the decades ahead.

The nature of economic reform
The new reforms under P.V. Narasimha Rao were essentially a continuation of the liberalization process introduced by Rajiv Gandhi from 1985 onwards. He had emphasized international technology transfers and domestic technology development as the key to modernization.

Since cutting down the Indian bureaucracy seemed a hopeless task, Rajiv Gandhi attempted instead to circumvent the bureaucracy in order to speed up the licensing of new industries or of joint industrial ventures with overseas firms. There were other liberalization measures adopted by Rajiv Gandhi that were intended to attract foreign investments, especially those that carried a foreign exchange-generating potential.[7] These piecemeal reforms and liberalization schemes under both Indira Gandhi and Rajiv Gandhi produced an average economic growth rate of about 5% since the mid-1970s. This was a considerable improvement from the average 3% that prevailed in the 1960s and early 1970s, often derisively referred to as the fatal 'Hindu rate of growth'.

The new reforms introduced since June 1991 were sudden and far reaching compared to those of the previous two Congress governments. The Rao government abolished the industrial licensing system, the scourge and despair of private-sector industrialists.[8] Indeed, post-independent India had been nicknamed 'The Licensing [or Permit] Raj' by its domestic critics. (Licences, however, are still required in those industries which may carry strategic value or generate hazardous effects or environmental damage.) Likewise, the Monopoly Regulation Act was considerably loosened by the Rao government. Firms no longer needed to obtain prior approval for new production, mergers or expansion of production. Most significantly, foreign corporations were entitled to own 51% equity in their Indian subsidiaries – even more in the case of special industries which generated exports or contributed to essential economic development goals. The Indian government also designated 34 industrial sectors which would be given automatic clearance for foreign investors.[9]

The reforms were welcomed by the West and world bodies such as the International Monetary Fund (IMF) and the World Bank. Within the first six months, seven major foreign collaborations with Indian firms worth Rs 1,100 *crores* ($440m) were approved.[10] Clearly, the actual investment value of these high-profile joint ventures was not as significant as the reputation and visibility of the collaborators themselves. The foreign firms included General Motors, Ford Motors, General Electric and Coca Cola of the US, Gerb and BMW of Germany and Buhler of Switzerland. Earlier, an agreement had been reached with Suzuki of Japan for expanding the production of the Suzuki–Maruti car in India. Donor nations also increased their aid commitments from $6.7bn in 1991–92 to $7.2bn for the year 1992–93, perhaps as a reward and incentive for further reform.[11]

However, there was little progress in the move towards privatization in India. Unlike Pakistan, which had put all its 100-plus public-sector undertakings on the auction block, Prime Minister Rao has been hesitant to move too quickly in the direction of privatization. There were fears that such a move would lead to extensive corruption charges and political recriminations (as has proved to be the case in Pakistan), and that it could produce a sudden political backlash from left-wing politicians and from the millions of workers in these public enterprises.[12] Consequently, few of the 260 public-sector undertakings corporations employing 2.3 million people were privatized during the first year of Rao's tenure. Instead, the emphasis has been on restructuring the undertakings, to be followed by a gradual transition to privatization through government disinvestment. Initially, 900m shares of 30 public-sector undertakings, were sold to other public-sector banks and financial institutions.[13] In 1992, however, 400m shares of eight major public-sector undertakings were auctioned to prospective investors in the private sector.

Needless to say, restructuring also meant eliminating inefficient production methods by cutting back on costly over-employment. With the prospect of large-scale lay-offs looming in the next few years, the Indian government allocated about $100m in 1991 to finance an employee retraining programme called the National Renewal Fund.[14] By the end of 1991, at least 60 public-sector units employing more than 400,000 people had been identified as chronic loss-making enterprises needing immediate restructuring or elimination. The total cost of restructuring these public sector undertakings was estimated at about $2.4bn.

The Congress government's economic reform movement in India has become cautious and hesitant for what appear to be political rather than economic reasons. Even those who advocate the shift from socialism to private capitalism suggest that reforms in India should be implemented slowly rather than suddenly. This would be contrary to the recommendation of Professor Jeffrey Sachs of Harvard University who suggested that the former eastern European communist governments were better off taking the 'bitter pill' approach, that is, suffering some extreme hardships in the short term for the sake of lucrative long-term gain. Therefore, should India plunge headlong into the free-market capitalist system instead of trying to make a gradual transition? Sach's argument was that a half-hearted approach was more likely to prolong the disadvantages of state socialism without gaining the benefits of private-sector capitalism. And the cautious approach was more likely to give opponents time to marshall political support to thwart the reform movement.

The increasingly cautious and hesitant policy of the Rao government was reflected in the Prime Minister's speech to the 44th meeting of the National Development Council in New Delhi in May 1992. Rao declared that the market mechanism could not be the 'sole vehicle' of development, and it and planning should be complementary to each other.[15] The market, according to the Indian prime minister, had limitations which would have to be supplemented by direct state intervention. In particular, he argued that state planning was necessary to take care of the poor and the downtrodden 'who are for the most part outside the market system and have little asset endowment to benefit from the natural growth of the economy'.

In sum, the overall nature of Indian reforms appears to be threefold. First, there will be no new public-sector undertakings or expansion, but these will continue temporarily as restructured units. Second, privatization will occur through a slow process of government disinvestment whereby the shares of public-sector undertakings will be auctioned periodically thereby diluting government ownership. Third, India will remove all obstacles to foreign and domestic private-sector investments and industrial expansion through the elimination of licences and permits.

Initial results and consequences of reform
The results of the reforms thus far have been mixed.[16] The failure to produce spectacular results was also largely due to the worldwide recession which had begun to hit the Indian economy. National expectations of the reforms were also much too high, and a year was hardly sufficient time to produce results. By mid-1992, doubts were raised about the effects of the reforms.

On the negative side, the growth of Indian gross domestic product (GDP) had declined to 1.5% in 1991–92, the year of the new reforms.[17] This compared to GDP growth rates of 9.4% in 1988–89, 6% in 1989–90 and 5.6% in 1990–91. Inflation, which was supposed to have been brought down from 12% to single digit figures, continued to hover at around 10–12%. On the positive side of the balance sheet, the annual fiscal deficit had been brought down from 8.4% of the GDP in 1990–91 to 6.5% in 1991–92, and to 5% in the current budget of 1992–93.[18] Although exports had declined from $18.1bn in 1990–91 to $17.8bn in 1991–92, the trade deficit had come down to $1.6bn through a cutback in imports. The foreign exchange reserves had increased from $1.3bn in 1990 to $5.4 bn in 1991. As is evident, most of these positive changes had taken place before the new reforms had been implemented. However, by late 1992 the Indian economy had begun to show signs of modest recovery.[19] The inflation-adjusted predicted growth for 1992–93 had risen to 4% on the basis of current monthly growth rates, and inflation had been brought down to 8% in August 1992.

The major reaction to the economic reforms has been the predictable opposition from trade unions representing public-sector corporation employees. National one-day strikes were called in November 1991 and again in June 1992. Both strikes were only partial successes.[20] Opposition groups, especially socialists in the *Janata Dal*, alleged that the Rao government had sold out to the World Bank and the IMF under pressure instead of pursuing an independent economic policy.

A more serious problem that sprung up in 1992 was a stock-market scandal where brokers and bankers colluded in using large amounts of bank deposits to speculate on the country's stock markets.[21] Several major banks and financial institutions in India faced huge losses including three foreign banks, the Australian ANZ Grindlays, the British

Standard Chartered Bank and the American Citibank. The financial scam was made possible by faults within the Indian banking and stock-market systems, and was probably exposed only because of the new economic openness introduced by the reforms. But the economic liberalization of the Rao government has been blamed by opposition politicians and critics for encouraging private greed and corruption.

Opposition to liberalization has been voiced occasionally and quietly by Indian industrialists and businessmen as well by those who are concerned about foreign competition that may be unfair or even impossible to cope with. Large Indian conglomerates such as Birlas and Tatas would like to control the entry of foreign competition. Small firms are fearful of being driven out of the marketplace.

By mid-1992, the Rao government seemed determined to proceed with the reforms. According to Finance Minister Manmohan Singh, the reforms will take about three to five years to show significant results. Even then it is unlikely that the growth rate will considerably exceed the average 5–6% growth rate of the 1980s. However, as Manmohan Singh pointed out, 'India cannot solve its problems of poverty and underdevelopment by going the command economy type of route where you find so much corruption, so much mismanagement, and there will neither be growth nor social justice. The economy cannot be run in the way we used to run it in the 1950s and 1960s and early 1980s'.[22]

The prospects for stability and development
External threat perceptions have been overshadowed by increasing internal violence and armed ethnic separatist movements. Many of the ethnic grievances provoking the rise in internal violence may be traced to rising economic expectations and despair. An Indian journalist, Prem Shankar Jha, summed up the basic problem of India as follows:

> Movements of insurrection are springing up all over the country like toadstools after rain. Most are as yet tiny, but have acquired an importance out of all proportion to the numbers involved because of the AK-47 rifle. The protest is not directed so much at the Indian state as that the state offers the insurrectionists no future within it. For this the very slow growth of the modern industrial and commercial sectors of the economy for 30 years after independence, its inefficient use of capital and the fewness of jobs created are directly to blame. As a result, every insurrectionary group from Punjab to Assam, from Kashmir to Tamil Nadu, is spearheaded by students and the educated unemployed. Slow economic growth has imperilled the polity, but today the opposite is also happening. The increasing weakness of the Center is making it more and more difficult to take harsh economic investment, increase its efficiency, and thereby hasten the rate of job creation in the modern sector.[23]

India's foreign and defence policies, and its domestic security and economic policies, have become much more interrelated and interdependent than in past decades. Rapid economic growth and a fair distribution of wealth will have an important bearing on resolving various domestic ethnic conflicts and separatist movements. Defence programmes will need to be cut back substantially to redirect more resources, especially foreign exchange, to the needs of economic development. And India will need to persevere with its economic reforms despite some initial setbacks. The economic dividends that are expected to accrue from the reforms will not be seen in the first year of its implementation, especially in the midst of the present worldwide recession. As noted earlier, the economy had already shown signs of revival by autumn 1992.

With the end of the Cold War era, closer ties with the United States and the West were perceived as essential for building up India's defence capabilities and for encouraging greater Western investments in India. No doubt, military ties with the US may prove useful, given the continuation of old conflict issues in South Asia and the continuing arms race in the region and beyond. Military collaboration with the United States may lower India's security risks within the subcontinent and bring about greater stability in the wider region from the Horn of Africa to the Strait of Malacca. But the expected pay-offs in terms of American weapons and military technology transfers to India do not appear likely to take place in the short run.

The continuing drive by the Indian Ministry of External Affairs to forge a new Indo-Russian treaty makes much less sense in the 1990s. Against whom would this treaty be directed? Apart from some mutual concerns about the future of the Muslim Central Asian republics, the two countries have few common strategic interests. Russia may still be a useful source for the purchase of cheap weapons, but these will have to be paid for in hard currency anyway at the maximum price Moscow is able to extract. A treaty will not obtain any special concessions for India on the purchase prices.

Half-hearted efforts to salvage the Non-Aligned Movement in India and abroad make even less sense in the 1990s. The meeting of various NAM leaders in Djakarta in September 1992 displayed a general lack of purpose and direction. Non-alignment can play little part in a world without opposing military blocs, and in a world which is characterized primarily by the division between rich and poor nations. Besides, India belongs to the group of poor countries and must seek negotiating and bargaining strategies jointly with other developing countries. India cannot be non-aligned between North and South. On other regional conflict issues in the former Soviet republics, in the former Yugoslavia, in the Horn of Africa and in Cambodia, the policy option for India is either to become involved or not involved. However, a policy of non-involvement would not be the same as the old non-alignment policy pursued during the Cold War.

Another hangover from the past is India's nuclear policy, where there has been little change. Perhaps it is time that India made a choice instead of sitting on the fence. Either India overtly embarks on a nuclear weapons programme and accepts the economic sanctions by the Western community that are bound to follow, or India should go ahead and sign the Nuclear Non-Proliferation Treaty (NPT). The traditional policy of 'maintaining the option' provides India with no deterrence against China or against a covert nuclear weapons programme in Pakistan. Perhaps nuclear weapons are intended to achieve great-power status. Thus, if India cannot obtain the respect of the West because it lacks economic influence, then this may be obtained through the display of its nuclear power. But the economic losses that it may suffer from such a policy may not be offset by the dubious intangible gains it may make in international prestige.

Without doubt, the greatest threat that India faces in the 1990s comes from within its borders. Armed separatist movements threaten to destroy the integrity of the state and to undermine the country's democratic system which has survived numerous crises since independence in 1947. After decades of fighting insurgencies in the border states and regions, it should have become apparent by now that there can be no purely military solutions to the problems of internal conflict. Only negotiated political solutions may avoid armed violence at home and bring about long-term stability. In particular, given the existence of several religious, linguistic, caste and tribal groups in India, the political structure and process may have to be drastically overhauled. Greater decentralization of political and economic power, and more confederal structural arrangements, may prove to be the necessary formula for solving the problems of internal security.

India's perseverance with democracy since independence may not be the only or main reason why the rest of the major states of South Asia turned democratic. Whatever the other reasons, by the early 1990s, all the states of South Asia had democratically elected governments, a situation found perhaps only in western Europe. It may be true that the East and South-east Asian countries were able to obtain high and sustained rates of economic growth because of the discipline provided by authoritarian regimes. But democracy enabled India to air the grievances of its myriad ethnic groups and thereby relieved the political pressure on the government and administration. Freedom of expression and of the electoral process provided outlets for frustration and despair. Democracy raised the hope that economic conditions could eventually be altered through the peaceful change of governments and leaders at the ballot box. India is more likely to survive as a union if its economy grows at an average of 7–8% per annum in a democratic capitalist system than at 10–12% in an authoritarian capitalist system. The trade-offs in terms of security and stability would appear to be worthwhile. With the end of the Nehru dynasty, the new Congress government has promised change and results.

Notes

[1] See the chapters by Nancy Jetley and Gowher Rizvi on the domestic dimensions of security in Barry Buzan and Gowher Rizvi (eds), *South Asian Security and the Great Powers* (London: Macmillan, 1986), pp. 37–92.

[2] There have been several reports and analyses on the dispute between India and the United States over the enforcement of 'Super 301' legislation. For a recent report, see *India Abroad*, 20 December 1991. For the official Indian viewpoint on the Russian rocket sale to India, see the press release by the Indian Embassy in Washington of 8 May 1992, 'Indian Import of Rocket Engine From Russia: Background and Facts'. For further Indian discussions on the Russian rocket sale, see *The Hindu*, 26 April 1992; *The Times of India*, 4 May 1992; and *India Abroad*, 22 May 1992. For a general assessment, see Manoj Joshi, 'Present Level of Indo-US Ties', *India Abroad*, 26 June 1992.

[3] These figures were obtained from the economic section of the IISS in London. The comparable figure for Turkmenistan was $3,020, for Kyrgyzstan it was $2,043, for Azerbaijan $1,850 and for Uzbekistan $1,630. See also Maqbool Ahmad Bhatty, 'Prospects for Cooperation with Central Asia', *The Nation* (Lahore), 8 October 1991. According to Bhatty, 'the Central Asian republics have relatively advanced economies, compared to ours [Pakistan], with an average per capita income 6 to 7 times higher than that of Pakistan'.

[4] Some Indian reports, confirmed by Pakistani analysts in Islamabad, showed that initial Pakistani overtures about Islamic ties were rebuffed by the Central Asian republics who indicated their preference for the secular ideology that they had become accustomed to as part of the Soviet Union. They were also insistent that they do not wish to see an Islamic fundamentalist regime replace the Najibullah regime in Kabul. See the report by Vinod Sharma, 'Afghan Stalemate May Turn Republics Hostile to

Pakistan', *Hindustan Times*, 10 January 1992. See also the reports in the *International Herald Tribune*, 26 November 1991, and *The Independent* (London), 27 April 1992.

[5] See *India Today*, 15 March 1992. Voter turnout for the 1992 Punjab election was only 25–30% with the urban areas showing a higher 40% turnout. In the rural areas, the voter turnout was only 15%.

[6] This highlights and elaborates on a view suggested by Prem Shankar Jha in his article, 'The Perilous Politics of Economic Reforms', *India Abroad*, 17 July 1992.

[7] See Alan Heston, 'India's Economic Reforms: The Real Thing?', *Current History*, vol. 91, no. 563, pp. 113–16.

[8] *Ibid.*, p. 115.

[9] Interview with Finance Minister Manmohan Singh, *India Today*, 31 July 1992.

[10] *Hindustan Times*, 14 January 1992.

[11] See *India Abroad*, 27 September 1991, and 3 July 1992.

[12] *Financial Times*, 19 and 21 November 1991.

[13] *India Abroad*, 2 October 1992.

[14] *Daily News* (Colombo), 21 January 1992.

[15] *The Times of India*, 23 May 1992.

[16] For various Indian assessments, see Subir Roy, 'Future of Reforms', *The Times of India*, 20 July 1992; and Shankar Jha, *op. cit.* in note 6.

[17] *The Times of India*, 14 July 1992.

[18] See I. Gopalkrishnan, 'Doubts Raised on Reform's Pace', *India Abroad*, 10 July 1992.

[19] See Suman Dubey, 'Indian Economy Shows Signs of Recovery', *The Wall Street Journal*, 8 September 1992.

[20] See the *Financial Times*, 21 November 1991; and *India Abroad*, 26 June 1992.

[21] See Rajendra Bajpai, 'India's Reform Keeps Bumping Along', *International Herald Tribune*, 23 July 1992; and the special report in *India Today*, 31 May 1992.

[22] *India Today*, 31 July 1992.

[23] Shankar Jha, *op. cit.* in note 6.

The Regional Impact of a Reforming India

DR STEPHEN P. COHEN

With the end of the Cold War, regional powers such as India appear to have assumed greater importance on the world map. This is partly an optical illusion: India, Iraq, Vietnam, Iran and other 'emerging' or 'middle' powers were always key players in their respective regions. Occasionally, their entanglement with larger states propelled them onto the global stage. But they have never ceased to be important, at least in proportion to their ambitions and their neighbours' anxieties. Three things have changed instead.

First, Western strategists now look at the ex-colonial world through new eyes. Some see an emerging threat to the industrialized world, some see a drain on their foreign-aid budgets and some (especially in Europe) see the foreshadowing of future ethnic strife, separatism and the revival of religious passions in their own region.

Second, the leaders of the significant regional powers are both pleased and uneasy with their new prominence. They fear becoming targets, like Iraq, almost as much as they previously resented being ignored and stereotyped by the former superpowers. But they, also, must come to grips with the regional origins of their insecurity. Not all – in South Asia, hardly any – regional conflicts were Cold War-induced. Further, the end of the Cold War has actually eliminated some of the mechanisms used to contain regional conflict.

Finally, there is a sharpened awareness of the non-military dimensions of security, including the problems of maintaining multi-ethnic states in an era of schism and separatism, greater concern over the spread of missiles and nuclear weapons and a revived interest in fostering democratic values. India ranks high in each of these three areas.

In the current context of shifting regional and non-regional perceptions, and the broadening of security concerns, it is difficult to speculate about the future. But India's recent past and its long history provide clues to the directions in which Delhi could move in the post-Cold War era.[1]

The changed international order

The breakdown of bipolarity and the collapse of the Soviet Union came as a shock to Indians, and their reassessment of the changing international order has been slower than that of other major powers. This is partly because India had four governments in less than three

years, but is more because of the orientation of Indian strategic thinking around the notion of a world divided among great powers. Nehru's
'non-alignment' was literally defined by the competition between
America and the former Soviet Union, but it had its roots in the
Congress Party's decision to go to jail during the Second World War
rather than support either the Allies or the Axis. Further, the way in
which the Cold War ended surprised the Indian strategic community.
They had assumed that both superpowers would moderate their behaviour and come to an agreement. And finally, the apparent triumph of
free-market economies and the failure of state-guided economic systems came as an unpleasant surprise: Indians had long been told by
their leaders that their mixed economy – neither communist nor capitalist – was a model for others.

The effort to recast India's policies has been complicated by two
internal developments. First, foreign policy bipartisanship has broken
down, partly as a result of the emergence of new political forces in
India itself – especially the growth of a Hindu revivalist movement.
Second, there is renewed concern over economic growth. Indians had
long prided themselves on their steady, but unspectacular, growth rate,
and derided the distorted consumer economies of ex-colonies that had
become dependent on outside investment and technology. But looking
to the East, rather than to the West, Indian leaders have discovered that
states such as South Korea, Thailand, Malaysia and Taiwan – all of
which were far behind India 40 years ago – have thriving economies
and have actually increased their independence. Further, most of these
states are more democratic than they were 40 years ago.

Renascent Hinduism and economic reform are essentially domestic
in origin. Their impact on foreign policy will be unpredictable, but it
has already been significant. A Congress government accommodated
the Hindu-oriented Bharatiya Janata Party, and opened an embassy in
Israel in early 1992. The same government has moved with astonishing
speed to accommodate international lending authorities by
deregulating and opening up the Indian economy. It has also significantly cut defence spending.

Under the influence of these domestic changes, as well as the
transformed international system, the Delhi-centred strategic community is in the midst of a national debate over security policy. The
following summarizes current and emerging assessments in order of
descending importance to the Indian strategic community.

Pakistan: the comprehensive threat
When the British quit South Asia, Indian nationalists were unable to
prevent the creation of Pakistan. To virtually all Indian strategists, this
was a British betrayal: it broke up the strategic unity of the subcontinent that – albeit intermittently – goes back 2,000 years to the first
Mauryan Empire.

Pakistan has been accepted by most Indians as an unfortunate fact of life, but they can also imagine what India would be like had partition not taken place. A united India would be more populous and powerful than China; it would have an industrial establishment that would place it about fourth or fifth in the world; and its borders would reach from the mouth of the Persian Gulf to South-east Asia. Such a state would not be a mere regional power, but would be one of the world's two or three great nations. It might have been a member of the Security Council, and would have been in a position to balance both Soviet and Chinese power. Today, it would be able to balance America or Japan and prevent them from abusing their currently dominant strategic and economic positions. For a leadership with strong historical memories, the notion of 'what might have been' remains important in shaping threat assessments. Thus, India–Pakistan relations are quite unlike relations between most other states. Pakistan's creation not only meant a reduction in Indian power, but much of that power has been diverted to meet the threat of an otherwise unimportant regional competitor.

Pakistan is also seen as ideologically threatening. A secular India, containing over 100 million Muslims, cannot view with equanimity a neighbouring Islamic state founded on the basis of religion. The creation of predominantly Muslim states in Central Asia, coupled with the rise of a revolutionary and Islamic Iran, is seen as somehow linked to the threat from Pakistan – and the enhanced relationship with Israel is one response to what is perceived as an extremist 'Islamic bloc'.

Conversely, some Pakistanis, encouraged by events in the former Soviet Union, believe that India itself is doomed to further partition and that it will not survive as an imperial entity. Thus, some Indians and some Pakistanis deny the legitimacy of the other state. This issue lies at the heart of India–Pakistan relations. A religious-based Pakistan threatens India's secularism; and a secular India (in which millions of Muslims live) threatens the religious basis of Pakistan's very existence. Further, even Indians who acknowledge the legitimacy of the Pakistani state believe that Islamabad has joined the United States, China and other countries in constraining India.

The threat to India from Pakistan – as perceived by the core Indian strategic community – is thus wide ranging and comprehensive. It is not merely territorial or economic, military or nuclear, but also ideological and theological. This makes it difficult for Indians to engage in serious negotiations or confidence-building measures with Pakistan, let alone to cooperate strategically with Islamabad (on, for example, Afghanistan or Central Asia, where both have significant interests and different assets). To do so would imply that Pakistan is a serious state and that its government is legitimate. Ironically, the restoration of democracy in Pakistan, coupled with Islamabad's admission of its nuclear weapons capability and strong evidence of its support for terrorists in Punjab and Kashmir, makes such a dialogue both necessary and even more distasteful. Delhi and Islamabad are drawn to talk to each other, and then repelled by the implications of the process.

Pakistan's bomb: threat or opportunity?

Nuclear proliferation has come to South Asia in one guise or another. Whether *de facto*, 'threshold', 'undeclared' or 'emergent' there is no question that India and Pakistan have the capacity to become nuclear-armed states, even if they have not yet acquired a nuclear capability – indeed, even if they never acquire or deploy nuclear weapons.[2] 1990 was a critical year in this nuclear drama. Leaders of both states looked down a gun barrel and saw radioactive clouds drifting over the Indus–Ganges plain.[3] There is now some consensus that a large-scale war will result not only in a stalemate, but a stalemate that will lead one state – and then both – to reconsider their declarations of non-nuclear status. This, in turn, raises the terrifying possibility of the actual use of nuclear weapons.

In this new nuclear relationship India and Pakistan face two major tasks. The first pertains to the whole range of questions associated with the maintenance of stability. This is not merely a problem of permissive action links, insensitive high explosives, acquiring secure second-strike forces and overcoming other technical challenges associated with being (or almost being) a nuclear weapons state. It also pertains to the link between nuclear weapons and other weapons.

Iraq used its chemical programme to protect its weaker nuclear programme. Baghdad assumed that Israel and the West could be deterred by the threat of chemical war from attacking its more serious nuclear infrastructure. The problem is somewhat different for the two South Asian states: they have achieved nuclear programmes, but only weak chemical and biological ones. However, their armies are more professional and better led than Iraq's. In their case, they must develop a strategic doctrine which somehow links weapons of mass destruction to conventional arms in such a way that the armed forces themselves accept their more limited role. This is particularly difficult in Pakistan, which is why nuclear weapons were so attractive in 1972 to Zulfiqar Ali Bhutto, then looking for ways to reduce the army's influence. Would the military allow nuclear targeting to rest exclusively in civilian hands? Probably yes, in India, but certainly not in Pakistan. President Zia was asked, just before his death, who in the military would control the use of nuclear weapons, especially if he were to leave office. The air force, which might be expected to deliver them, or the politically more trustworthy army? Or a combination of the two – with what consequences for tactical flexibility and site security? He evaded giving a reply, but was aware that nuclearization – or near-nuclear status – raised a whole cluster of strategic, doctrinal, technical and political problems.

However, it is also true that quite apart from the need to balance each other's programmes, regional nuclear hawks argue that nuclearization provides a remarkable opportunity for Indian and Pakistani policy-makers to advance important interests, and especially to demand admission to the ranks of the regional great powers. A nuclear India would also feel more confident in addressing the United States and China as near-equals, and even in demanding a subsequent general reduction in nuclear arms. The nuclear lobby does not mind if Pakistan achieves nominal equality with Beijing and a declining Moscow and Washington. Balancing this, India (and Pakistan) must calculate the costs to their present economic reform programmes should the Western powers and Japan punish them for flaunting the global movement towards denuclearization.[4]

China: the uncertain threat
China is no longer seen as a serious political or military threat to India. The Indian strategic community is impressed with China's economic progress, but feels that its own research and scientific institutions, coupled with India's greater access to Western technology, will eventually put India ahead. Further, it argues that Beijing's centralized communist government is inflexible and out of touch with reality.

Yet China continues to worry New Delhi. It provides military assistance to India's neighbours (not only Pakistan, but also Nepal, Bangladesh and Myanmar), sometimes with unpredictable results. The Indian response to China's weapons sales to Nepal, for example, triggered off a national uprising against the king and led to the democratization of that country; on the other hand, Beijing's assistance to the Burmese generals has emboldened them to move against various non-Burmese groups, leading to a crisis with Bangladesh. Indians are unsure about the best way to counter these regional interventions by China.

Indians are also divided over their response to the Chinese nuclear programme, now that the Soviet Union is no longer present as a strategic counterweight. After the first Chinese test in 1964, India sought, and received, informal assurances from both the United States and the Soviet Union. It pursued its own nuclear programme at a moderate pace, secure in the belief that with both superpowers on Delhi's side, the Chinese would show restraint.

However, without such external support, India has begun to respond more directly to China's nuclear and missile programmes. When China acquired missiles, the Indians produced the *Agni* intermediate-range ballistic missile (IRBM), a 'technology demonstrator' of some sophistication. When China conducted a large nuclear test in mid-1992, India test-fired its second *Agni*. India will refrain from an overt weapons build-up if its relationship with China continues to improve and if Pakistan does not declare itself a nuclear weapons state. However, this policy is always subject to revision, and New Delhi's sheer military and technical capabilities are growing at a rate that would make a decision to increase arms technically easy and economically manageable. The barriers to a fully-fledged Indian programme (and to such a programme in Pakistan) are political, not technical or economic. Both regional states know that their new economic strategies would be at risk, and their access to advanced technology cut off, if they were suddenly to emerge as military nuclear powers. In the meantime, they continue a fitful dialogue on proliferation. India, in particular, is reluctant to talk about a regional arms control regime until it has prior assurances from the United States that such 'five-power' talks will not deteriorate into 'India-bashing'.

Smaller neighbours

Indian strategists claim that the South Asian regional structure confronts them with special problems. India's size and power make any comparison with Sri Lanka, Nepal or even Pakistan unrealistic. For many years, Jawaharlal Nehru sounded the theme that in the entire world only China was truly analogous to India: a great civilization embodied in a single country. Yet, India's neighbours are so fearful of Indian dominance that they constantly undercut Delhi. Of course, Indian strategists do not accept the legitimacy of these fears, and argue that New Delhi has been a benign regional power.[5] The reluctance of neighbouring states to accept India's leadership (and Pakistan's attempt to challenge it) weakens the 'natural' regional security structure.

From an Indian perspective the greatest weakness of Nepal, Sri Lanka, Bhutan and Bangladesh is that their regimes tend to be undemocratic, and hence anti-Indian; most Indians hold the Wilsonian view that the people of the region are sympathetic to India because of historic ties of culture, religion and language. This has inevitably created a number of overlapping ethnic groups in South Asia (Bengalis in Bangladesh and India, Kashmiris, Sindhis and Urdu speakers in India and Pakistan, Tamils in India and Sri Lanka, and Nepali speakers in Nepal and India, to mention only the largest). As Delhi sees it, the weak economies and corrupt, undemocratic regimes of these neighbours cause various groups to flee their homeland, and in some cases require India to provide refuge for democratic opposition groups. This view is strongly shared by Indian politicians in such border states as Assam, West Bengal, Bihar and Uttar Pradesh, where poor migrants from neighbouring Bangladesh and Nepal are economically threatening to local voters. Further, India's undemocratic neighbours tend to invite outside powers into the region, endangering regional security.

Finally, these states pose some limited strategic risk since they are suspected of trying to unite against India. This was the chief reason why New Delhi was suspicious of the South Asian Association for Regional Cooperation (SAARC). This was proposed by Bangladesh, but had its roots in Nepal's failed effort to be acknowledged as a 'Zone of Peace', a concept firmly rejected by India. New Delhi has treaties or agreements with Nepal, Bangladesh, Bhutan and Sri Lanka that add up to a regional security arrangement – almost an Indian Monroe Doctrine – and is wary of efforts by any of these states to acquire greater freedom of manoeuvre. Thus, one condition attached to SAARC was that it should neither deal with bilateral issues nor include any security or defence matters.

Washington and Moscow
While it is unsurprising that most Indians were disconcerted by the end of bipolarity, it was remarkable that many intellectuals and policy-makers blamed America for having 'won' the Cold War. Indian strategists now warn of the perils of unipolarity and retain a belief in the enduring realities of balance-of-power politics. Yet India has realistically moved closer to the United States, if for no other reason than to deflect and guide American power, to 'co-opt' Washington on issues of paramount importance to Delhi.[6]

Indians are deeply divided today over relations with the United States. One large group believes that Washington is out to encircle and undercut New Delhi. Why? Because India is an independent power that has refused to join any American alliance, and is willing to mount a principled challenge to America. India's leadership of the Non-Aligned Movement (NAM) is, according to this view, a threat to American expansionism, and New Delhi must be cut down, or at least countered with American surrogates, such as China and Pakistan.

However, a group of Indian pragmatists have emerged, who reject the shibboleths of the past. They have, since 1985, been arguing that India cannot advance economically unless it develops close ties with the United States – which they regard as the world's leading industrial and economic power. They write and speak of economic and strategic cooperation between the world's two largest democracies, but have not been able to articulate persuasive proposals and projects for this.

As for the former Soviet Union, Delhi's foreign-policy establishment would like to retain as much of a relationship with it as possible. The Indian armed forces are still dependent on former Soviet Union-origin equipment and spare parts, and India would like to acquire both military and dual-use technology. However, the greatest importance of Russia lies in its potential revival as a strategic ally, and even as a balancer both to China and an unpredictable United States.

Indian regional policy: the 'Indira Doctrine' and beyond
Over a thousand years ago, there were extensive Indian empires in much of South-east Asia, covering all of present-day Cambodia. Earlier, the influence of Buddhism had spread from India northwards through Tibet into China and Japan, southwards to Ceylon and on to much of South-east Asia. This record of cultural and political expansionism (and the practices of the British, who recruited Indian labour for plantations and factories from East Africa to Fiji) has left behind a range of important interests. These include the rights of citizens of Indian origin across the Indian Ocean region; control over access points to the Indian Ocean; access to the untapped natural resources in

the area, including sea-bed mining; and the maintenance of Indian political and cultural influence in countries with historic ties to the subcontinent. From an Indian perspective, the Asian and Indian Ocean regions offer a chance to rebuild and exploit ancient historical, cultural and economic ties.

For many years the notion of developing a doctrine or strategy to guide Indian foreign policy in this region was out of the question. India lacked the resources to project its power beyond its immediate neighbourhood, and it continued to see Pakistan and China – and, for some, the United States – as positively hostile to the Indian state. Indian strategic thinking remained intensely defensive in outlook, focusing on the internal security of India itself – particularly the strain produced by respectable but very uneven social change and economic growth.

However, with the defeat of Pakistan in 1970 things appeared to change. From the mid-1970s onwards, Indian policy-makers formulated a regional security doctrine that later acquired the label of 'Indira Doctrine'. Two principles were laid down: no foreign power should be allowed to cross the crest of the Himalayas; and India would consider the presence of or influence of an external power in the region as against its interests. In the light of India's inaction during the Soviet invasion of Afghanistan, the latter now seems peculiarly optimistic.

In two cases, however, the Indira Doctrine was vigorously applied. The first was Sri Lanka. While largely motivated by internal Indian considerations (the politics of the Indian state of Tamil Nadu), India's actual intervention in June 1987 was justified on the grounds that outside powers were about to gain a foothold in Sri Lanka. The other intervention, in the Maldives, was a genuine response to a crisis in Male.

The Indian strategic community has drawn several lessons from these interventions. There is unanimity on the effectiveness of the Maldive intervention, but the case of Sri Lanka has split Indian strategists. The army was furious over bad intelligence and political restrictions on its operations. Senior officers speak openly about their reluctance to become involved in Sri Lanka, or any similar situation, again. But many civilian strategists, while acknowledging the tactical problems faced by the army, argue that as a great regional power, India will have to intervene periodically in troubled neighbourhoods. Further, they argue that a truly great state must demonstrate its will and ability to use force, and that for this reason alone the Sri Lankan intervention must be regarded as a success.

Thus, while Indian strategic thinking is now in a state of contraction and reflection, the interests and the impetus behind the Indira Doctrine remain valid. The *idea* of intervention – where politically, morally and militarily justified – is still widely supported. The most recent case was the evacuation of nearly 100,000 Indian citizens from the Gulf region just before the war began. This technical *tour de force* was civilian-managed, but indicates an ability to project power considerable distances under the right circumstances. Given the likelihood of future opportunities for intervention (both in the immediate ring of weak neighbours, and in the smaller Indian Ocean region states, especially those with significant Indian ethnic minorities), it is very likely that the Indira Doctrine – most certainly with a new name, and perhaps under multilateral auspices – will again be invoked before the decade is over.

Conclusions

Relations with Pakistan will remain at the centre of Indian security calculations for the remainder of this decade, although they have just undergone a major (nuclear) transformation. There is a good chance that the shared political and strategic interests of the two countries can be further explored. These include their nuclear programmes, their joint Kashmir problem and common environmental and economic interests. For this kind of dialogue to begin there will have to be a willingness to forget some aspects of the past. In the last eight months, such dialogues (conducted privately, although with both governments' approval) have started. They should be encouraged.

The case for a more coherent regional political structure, which would enable India and its neighbours to move ahead on a number of shared concerns, is self evident, but has been rejected by two generations of Indian strategists on the grounds that Delhi weakens its authority by engaging in regional (as opposed to bilateral) arrangements with its smaller neighbours. There are signs that this attitude is changing. First, 'regionalism' as a movement has produced concrete results, largely in the forum of SAARC. Terrorism, narcotics and some regional cultural and economic programmes have become SAARC subjects with no diminution of Indian sovereignty. Second, the wave of democratization that swept over South Asia may make it easier to engage in regional cooperation. India could be the *de facto* leader of the largest bloc of democratic peoples in the world. This will enhance, not degrade, India's reputation. Indeed, outsiders have looked with dismay on an India that has regarded itself as somehow threatened by Bangladesh or Nepal – states are known by the enemies they keep.

India maintains the world's third or fourth largest army and a substantial navy and air force. These forces were built up after 1962 with Western and Soviet assistance. With the end of Soviet aid, the quality of Soviet weapons in doubt as a result of the war in the Gulf, India's own arms factories unable to deliver modern equipment in large numbers and the cost of the most advanced Western equipment out of reach, the purpose as well as the performance of India's vast military–industrial complex is coming into question. A few defence professionals have suggested alternative ways of procuring weapons and maintaining armed forces. Some are studying national service schemes, others have questioned the value of India's vast paramilitary

forces, and nuclear advocates claim that India can have 'more rumble
for a rupee'. When coupled with the end of the Cold War and the
current interest in regional confidence-building measures, it is unlikely
that India's own military structure will remain unexamined. India
needs a modern military establishment, but the next five years could
see the first national debate in 25 years over the purpose, shape and use
of that force.

The experience, training and ideological inclinations of the Indian
strategic elite have provided them with few clues about how to conduct
complex diplomacy in a multipolar world. Nehru and successive generations of Indian leaders came to political maturity in a system of
strong global powers: first the British Empire; then the United States
and the former Soviet Union. The fabric of Indian foreign policy was
woven out of the struggle against the British and, recently, against
other 'neo-colonial' powers: the romantic and just struggle of the
victim against the strong and powerful. It is difficult for Indian politicians and policy-makers to avoid seeing the world as divided between
potential victims on the one hand, and dominant states on the other.
Neither they (nor anyone else, for that matter) have a clear role model
for a regional dominant power other than as a client of a superpower,
or a challenger to superpower incursions.

In the 1990s, however, some of the assumptions underlying Nehru's
vision of the world as made up of many cooperating states may be
valid. There is now the prospect of five or six major world powers,
each capable of exerting political, economic or military influence in
more than one region of the world. India is unique in this configuration
because it is the most powerful state of the next tier. Like China and
Russia, India abuts and influences several adjacent regions. Its cultural
power, entrepreneurial skills and scientific expertise extend around the
globe. Also, India's power is balanced: it not only commands considerable military force, but its economy is growing in size and sophistication; Indian cultural and political influence is strong in the Indian
Ocean region; and the quality of Indian leadership is high. In a more
fluid, complex and multipolar world, regional powers such as India
could assume new importance.

Yet there is little evidence that the present Indian strategic leadership has thought much about such a role. There is unanimous agreement that India *should* be a global power, but no model seems appropriate. The day has long since passed when India could aspire to the
role of balancer between the United States and the former Soviet
Union. India's position in NAM does not do justice to Indian capabilities and experience, and in any case NAM has become marginalized.
The Indian elite holds an expanded vision of their country's destiny,
but it remains to be seen whether they will turn vision into reality. This
uncertainty is what will make India such a problematic and interesting
power for the next several years.

Notes

[1] For a fuller exposition, see Stephen P. Cohen, 'India as a Great Power: Perceptions and Prospects', in Philip Oldenburg (ed.), *India Briefing, 1991* (Boulder, CO: Westview Press, 1991).

[2] The capacity/capability distinction is currently in vogue among Indian strategists. Its use serves a number of purposes, including that of claiming to be a nuclear or missile power without accepting the responsibilities of being one.

[3] Until recently, Indians and Pakistanis had devoted little or no thought to the consequences of a regional nuclear war. Those who were aware of them tended to be hawks, and it was in their interest to play down the consequences of a nuclear exchange. For an effort to model a regional nuclear war, see S. Rashid Naim, 'Aadhi Raat ke Baad [After Midnight]', in Stephen P. Cohen (ed.), *Nuclear Proliferation in South Asia: The Prospects for Arms Control* (Boulder, CO: Westview Press, 1991).

[4] I have addressed the coming crisis brought on by the extension of the Nuclear Non-Proliferation Treaty (NPT), and offered a way out that should meet everyone's core security concerns – helping India and Pakistan move to advanced defensive technologies, and assisting them in managing their conventional arms race in exchange for yielding on their military nuclear programmes. See 'A Way Out of the South Asia Arms Race', *Washington Post*, 28 September 1992.

[5] On balance, this is probably an accurate assessment. Historically, Indian expansionism has been cultural, not military or political. Indians seem content with this mode, which in some ways resembles the Chinese approach to its semi-Sinicized neighbours.

[6] For a discussion of the way in which both Washington and Delhi have adopted strategies of co-option towards each other, see Stephen P. Cohen, 'India's Role in the New Global Order: An American Perspective', a paper presented to the 3rd Indo-US Strategic Symposium, 21–23 April 1992 (Washington DC: National Defense University, forthcoming).

Europe and Asia: the Missing Link

FRANÇOIS GODEMENT

The role of Europe in Asian affairs is an issue of the past or the future, but not so much one of the present. This is even truer of a related question – the role of Asia in Europe.
There are several reasons for this. First, Europe, and even more so Asia, remain vague geopolitical concepts. Asia is made up of several subregions, and no international organization has ever encompassed any of them until the very recent advent of the Asia–Pacific Economic Cooperative (APEC). From the point of view of security, the fact that even subregional groupings with the West such as the South-East Asia Treaty Organization (SEATO) failed in the past, and that the US never went beyond the stage of bilateral defence treaties with Asian countries, does suggest something about the heterogeneity of the region.

THE LIMITS TO EUROPE
To describe Europe as diverse and vague may sound out of tune in the age of the Maastricht Treaty. Yet this is still the case, despite many Asian, and sometimes American, fears of a European bloc, and is especially so in the areas of foreign policy and security: how the Treaty, which includes the foundations for a future European security and foreign policy, will in fact evolve remains an open question.
Beyond the present 12 members of the European Community (EC), the very extension of Europe is geopolitically debatable. For a time after the eastern European 'revolutions' of 1989, it was tempting to stretch the concept of Europe all the way east to Kazakhstan and the so-called 'Maritime Provinces' of the Russian Federation on the Pacific. Was the European Community a much too restrictive designation, closing the door to its neighbours in central and eastern Europe? Was it unfair to exclude Russia? And was not Russia at the heart of the Commonwealth of Independent States (CIS) and therefore interlocked with its other members? This was the generous argument for the immediate, and theoretically boundless, 'widening' of the European concept, proposed at the same time that ministers in Brussels were 'deepening' the concept among its 12 existing members.
A number of difficulties, among them the Yugoslav crisis and fears about immigration, have put an end to this reasoning. It became apparent during the 1991 Gulf War that Europe could not have its own 'out-of-area' security policy. The Western European Union (WEU), revived in the 1990s, was supposed to address this matter. But the

predicament in the former Yugoslavia has demonstrated that Europe is still a long way from possessing a genuine and comprehensive security policy. Germany would subscribe to military intervention in the Balkans, but claims to be constitutionally prevented from participating in any such venture; the French, British and Italians (among others) may have the military means to intervene, but not the political will to carry the burden entirely on their shoulders. Thus the former Yugoslavia has not been brought any closer to Europe as a result of the tragic war there; rather, it seems to have become more distant. Given the present political situation in Europe, a country could be said to be European if there is no perceived risk of it going to war with another EC member; a country cannot be European (for example Turkey) if it is perceived as at risk of a conflict with another member. Likewise, it is becoming clear that the right of admission to Europe will be granted first to formerly neutral countries of the Cold War era (such as Austria and Sweden), and then to the most developed states in central and eastern Europe (the Czechs – though not the Slovaks – Hungary and possibly Poland). Thus, countries cannot join Europe in order to solve a problem; they may do so only if they have already solved it.

Given the very tight and integrative definition of Europe today, and the absence of a security arm, membership has to be carefully restricted. In European construction, defence comes last in practice. Security dialogues are a good thing while there is no actual conflict, but they are no substitute for a common defence policy when the conflict is already there. The existing nucleus of a Franco-German force, politically important as a test for the future, is certainly not the most likely organization to be chosen for 'out-of-area' interventions, including in the former Yugoslavia.

For all these reasons Europe has not only put a temporary brake on its external policies – for instance, no recent statement from any summit of European leaders mentions Asia in any form – but it has also receded into the management of its own problems. Because of the excessive ambitions ascribed to Europe, it sometimes looks inactive, indecisive or ungenerous instead, particularly in the case of the former Yugoslavia. This, however, is not so in terms of the large amounts of aid committed by Europe to Africa, eastern Europe and the CIS; however, its present inability to act successfully in the Yugoslav conflict will diminish the impact of Europe's human rights efforts in other parts of the world.

THE LIMITS TO EUROPEAN EXTERNAL ACTION

In spite of disagreements over the Maastricht Treaty, and the beginning of federative action in some areas, if Europe becomes a union of independent nation-states they will maintain their own objectives and ideas. This is, of course, becoming less true of monetary policy, driven, with or without Maastricht, by the Deutsche Mark; and there are other specific areas (agriculture, environment, law) where decisions are practically withdrawn from the national level. Such, however, is certainly not the case with foreign policy, defence and the industrial and trade policies that contribute to the promotion of exports. In these areas, there is only symbolic European cooperation (such as the European Parliament's resolutions on human rights) or overlapping – and sometimes conflicting – representation by the EC and its member nation-states.

Some examples relate to Asia as well as to other areas. In spite of the existence of three or four Commissions in Brussels dealing with Asia, there is no common action being undertaken at the European level except on anti-dumping matters. There are in fact about 150 bureaucrats employed in Brussels in the anti-dumping department, but only one person is employed for European export promotion. This reflects the fundamental notion that Europe is first and foremost about passive legal integration, and only very remotely is there any attempt at a common strategy towards the outside world. In some well-known instances, the European Community has given preference to its rulings regarding internal market fairness and anti-trust regulations over coordinated industrial policy in areas of worldwide competition: especially so when the Commission disapproved the takeover of the De Havilland group by Aerospatiale. The explanation given by the Commission was that this takeover would have given Aerospatiale too dominant a position in the European market for small passenger planes (although other European producers, such as Fokker and British Aerospace, would still remain in the same field). In spite of the rigours of US anti-trust legislation, Boeing does not seem to have been hampered in the past by similar reservations. In this view, the EC seems to have achieved exactly what it has proclaimed to be its main goal since 1958: to be a mechanism for a unified and free market.

Although the Community does give development aid, it does not possess the means to run this aid on the ground. And in fact, when European member-states gathered in Tokyo with Japan, the United States and other nations to announce a very large assistance scheme for the United Nations Development Programme (UNDP) in Cambodia, the European representatives announced their contributions individually, and not collectively: yet taken together, European aid commitments, at $220m, were larger than the corresponding figures from Japan and the United States. The Community does not manage export credits or soft loans, and export promotion is only 'a matter of tokenism', as one EC official put it privately in July 1992: 'medical instruments in Singapore' at an export fair was the example cited.

External action at the European level therefore exists only sketchily. Europe does not possess the combination of executive and legislative action that allows the United States, for instance, to have 'Super 301'-type legislation to back up trade representatives at the government level. As of today, not only is the EC not a superstate, it is not even a state. Political or strategic discussions with Asian nations simply do not exist at the level that prevails between North America and Asia. This has nothing to do with either Asian openness or refusal to create balanced relations with Europe; it is a consequence of the present European construction model. The EC, for example, does not officially keep figures regarding European direct industrial investment in other regions of the world: this is done only at the national level, with considerably different accounting methods.

Another well-known feature of external action missing in Europe, and also largely at the level of member countries, is the existence of lobbies for action. There are in Brussels a good many Asian-based lobbies concerned with the internal workings of the EC and legislation controlling access to the market. But there are almost no European lobbies pushing for decisions in Asia: a major exception, as shall be seen, is the human rights and humanitarian lobby, if it can be so called.

AREAS OF EUROPEAN ACTION IN ASIA

Of course, the above remarks are not accurate in the case of the activities of many European Community representatives, and the much greater role that the EC plays in some areas in Asia. The Community has opened diplomatic missions in Tokyo, Beijing, Hanoi and Seoul. It takes part in the Post-Ministerial Conference (PMC) dialogue after each Association of South-East Asian Nations (ASEAN) Conference. It has even created, in order to bridge the gap with China that has existed since 1989, a semi-official meetings format: every year after the United Nations General Assembly, the three foreign affairs ministers of the present, past and future presidencies of the European Community meet with the Chinese foreign affairs minister. And the EC–Japan dialogue, after years of mutual acrimony on trade relations, has produced its first results with an 'informal' agreement on export restraints on Japanese car manufacturers.

Perhaps more to the point, the diplomatic missions of the EC play a large role in trade and assistance relations. This is perhaps achieved more on a case-by-case basis than as a result of forward planning. A good case in point, for example, is action in China: the EC is concerned about Airbus sales in a country that buys 85% of its civilian planes from Boeing or Douglas. Nothing is simple, however, since Boeing planes sometimes come equipped with Rolls Royce – that is, European – engines; conversely, advertising by a regional Chinese airline (China Eastern) takes care to emphasize that its new Airbuses come with 'American CFM engines'. The Community is concerned about the fact that American action over intellectual property rights and shipping privileges in China seems to be getting better results than any one else. But it will not be involved in any of the industrial joint ventures established by European firms on the Chinese market.

The areas in which European Community actions are truly important are probably threefold. Respect for human rights is one, although this is not unique to Europe since US administrations, sometimes encouraged by Congress, have also been very active. National reactions to breaches of human rights are often coordinated, or paralleled, by reactions at the European Parliament or Commission level. Whether in Afghanistan, Cambodia or East Timor, humanitarian action by Europe has been essential. In the case of East Timor, the gradual change of policy by the Indonesian government over its information and treatment of the issue has probably been motivated by European action more than by any other factor, including constant Australian campaigning. The European-level discussions probably help overcome the commercial competition factor among members in major cases, such as China in 1989–90. Although there has been official restraint in view of the existing ASEAN consensus, the situation in Myanmar has also been the subject of European declarations and communications to states in the region.

Development assistance is another striking area. The commitment to Cambodia undertaken by members of the European Community in 1992 has already been mentioned. The example of China – still a 'South' country in spite of its recent progress – shows that, in this area, European aid can be both generous and independent of commercial considerations. The EC contributes about $55m to development aid in China,[1] including a large powdered-milk project that will require $60m over five years. A decision made at the Lisbon European Summit in 1992 commits another part of this sum to agricultural projects in the poorest regions of China, such as Xinjiang province. These projects place heavy emphasis on technical transfer and know-how. Both a biology and a cereal-crop yield centre have been established. The first example of technical help to China is of course the European management centre established in Beijing in 1985. The concern at the time was to help China increase its exports, a concern which seems to have been well met since the Chinese trade surplus with EC countries was in excess of $10 billion in 1991. Europe, in fact, takes a more forthcoming attitude to China's admission to the General Agreement on Tariffs and Trade (GATT). According to a reliable source, it will ensure that China is admitted to GATT '15 minutes before Taiwan', thus hoping for greater leverage on the trade policies of both.

Other features of European unity occasionally pertain to Asia. In Franco-German relations, for example, a degree of formal diplomatic cooperation has been decided. Outer Mongolia, therefore, is the first country in which there is a joint diplomatic mission for both countries, manned by French and German diplomats together.

The above examples of European action regarding Asia do not deny Europe's fundamental limitations in this area. Yet are Europe's trade and investment links in Asia equally limited? Certainly, if one takes into account expectations about these links. Probably not, if one starts from present-day realities, at the national or company level. Almost all European countries have increased the relative importance of their trade and investment with Asia since 1980. For the first half of the decade, this contrasted with the declining relative figures of US exports and investment in the same area. Countries such as China, Japan, Taiwan and Korea developed economic policies, directed towards Europe – and even more so after major trade controversies with the United States and the decline in the value of the dollar in 1985 undermined their financial savings abroad. But in the second half of the 1980s, the United States caught up again. Growth rates for Asia–Pacific imports from Japan, the United States and Europe do place Europe in the lead, but from a much lower starting point; in direct investment, yearly growth rates over the same period (1985–90) for Europe are +13.2%, which is still behind the US level of +14.5% and the Japanese level of +19.3%. In absolute levels of exports and direct investment, Europe in 1990 still came third after the United States and Japan.[2] At the company level, oil companies excepted, very few European firms or multinationals have a major commitment in the Asian region; there are a few examples like Thomson, the French electronics firm, that has staked its electronic consumer goods strategy on more than 50% Asian-based production. Typically, globally minded European firms will aim at ensuring, sometimes through local participation, a minimal (not more than 5%) but assured share of Asian markets: this is probably the case for about 500 large European firms. Some ventures, with a relatively limited initial cost, have been very rewarding: the Volkswagen joint venture in Shanghai is now officially the most profitable foreign operation in that country, with a profit for 1991 slightly under $200m (European car manufacturers as a whole have benefited from the Japanese manufacturers' reluctance to launch production in China). More often, the choice of locally strong partners will ensure that competition is limited: the problem with this strategy is that it limits future growth within Asian markets. All this explains why, in spite of the relative slow-down of US multinationals in Asia, their absolute position is still much stronger than that of their European counterparts.

Before looking to the future, it should be emphasized, however, that the nature of the European presence in Asia, as well as the future importance of the European market, represents huge advantages for Asian nations. In almost no area, except trade legislation within Europe, is Europe dealing from a position of superiority, or swapping political and strategic favours against trade compromises. European political attitudes – mainly on human rights issues – may be of deep concern to some Asian governments, but they seldom fit into any pre-established strategy, and merely express, therefore, the sensitivity of European public opinion and concerned groups.

Furthermore, the above-mentioned reservations about Europe's present external role in Asia are not the final word on this topic. Europe is still in an unfinished state. Some of the criticism implied by its present lack of strategy may seem close to the spirit of Mrs Thatcher's Bruges Charter – an all-out liberal attack against European bureaucracy and superstate intervention. But most of the answers given today in Europe to these problems point out the need for more Europe, rather than less. What is particularly striking, in any case, is how far the true state of European affairs is from the popular image of three world trading blocs competing with each other. While there are certainly passive protectionist trends and groups in Europe, there are far fewer elements of united commercial and political strategy. Certainly far less so than in the United States, and even than in Japan, where firm concentration and the absolute weight of Japan's economy within Asia overshadows the Japanese government's traditional caution and hesitation.

ISSUES FOR EUROPE IN ASIA
There is no dearth of issues relating to security between Europe and Asia. They can be categorized in three different groups: issues that clearly overlap the geopolitical borders of Europe and Asia; issues that serve to reinforce what is sometimes called the 'third side of the triangle' in the global relations of the Alliance, that is, Europe–Asia relations, complementing those of America–Asia and America–Europe; and issues of mutual interest that serve to improve relations between Europe and Asia.

In the first category falls the mutual participation of Europe and Asia in each other's affairs. Among European nations, France and Britain still have a geopolitical footing in the Asia–Pacific. France has a large maritime area in the South Pacific. Now that the political and diplomatic crisis of the mid-1980s has abated, France has suspended its nuclear testing and announced a moratorium and is anxiously waiting for other nuclear powers to follow suit. Diplomatic links with the South Pacific region have improved, and economic relations between New Caledonia, French Polynesia and such economies as those of Japan and Taiwan are increasing. Although historically the administration of these overseas territories has remained much too self-centred, this recent evolution points to longer-lasting relations with Asia. Within the necessary participation of the EC in various Asia–Pacific dialogues, France has a special claim for membership, if at a modest level, in Pacific dialogues and institutions such as APEC. Britain has important links with the region through Hong Kong, Malaysia and Singapore.

In the recent past, this has been balanced by Japan's interest in participating in the Conference on Security and Cooperation in Europe (CSCE). Although Japan's claim, or that of any other Asian country, to be part of the European continent-building process is of course weaker than that of either France or Britain regarding their actual foothold in the Pacific Basin, economic and technological realities suggest otherwise. In reality, both Japan and Korea's geopolitical interest and economic capacity to participate in the development of the CIS and eastern Europe qualify them for limited status within the very broad framework of the CSCE.

A second area of overlapping interest concerns security and arms control processes linked with the former Soviet bloc. The end of the Cold War and the disappearance of the Soviet factor have in fact slowed down the process of common awareness in this area. At the time of the intermediate-range nuclear forces (INF) negotiation, the swing factor of the Soviet medium-range missiles between Europe and Asia became an integrating factor in Europe and Asia's security concerns. It was certainly the main substantive point made by Japan at world summits from Williamsburg to Venice, although the Reagan administration was really the chief arbiter in these negotiations. But Europe's delaying of the process until a zero-option including Asia was decided certainly constituted a breakthrough.[3] Most outstanding issues involving proliferation or the disbanding of the former Soviet Union's military and nuclear potential are really global in nature. Issues such as nuclear reactor safety, waste disposal and the possible role of fast-breeders require discussion, however. Europe could also play a role in the gradual unwinding of the division and tension in the Korean peninsula, partly through the example of German reunification and because Germany has a special diplomatic position in both Koreas due to its own history. But also because European countries can still play a role in reorganizing both halves of Korea, and because a European contribution would balance fears about the interest of Japan and the United States in Korean affairs.

Among the issues belonging to the 'third side of the triangle' between Europe, the United States and Asia are issues of a presently global nature. Nuclear proliferation is a reality in South Asia, and could become one in North-east Asia. The future reform of the UN Security Council, with Japan's undeclared candidacy for a permanent seat, and Germany's recent announcement that its own claim would follow Japan's, obviously directly involves the regional order in Europe and Asia. This will test China, France and Great Britain's present attitude of 'wait and see', or unofficial opposition. But the actual solutions to this membership problem may involve a move to a more integrative regional order in Europe and Asia: Japan clearly cannot act as one of the world's policemen without much more understanding from other Asian countries; Germany's present constitutional and political contradictions, blatant in the Yugoslav crisis, clearly show that it would need some form of European association to exercise this responsibility. Former Italian head of government Giulio Andreotti's remark about an EC seat on the Security Council pointed in the same direction, even if it did not take into account the EC's present weakness as a security entity.[4] To dispel rumours, a spokesperson for the German Foreign Ministry confirmed on 3 August 1992 Germany's 'interest' in a permanent seat on the Council.

This leaves the third category of issues, namely areas where Europe and Asia can strengthen their mutual relationships without direct interference or influence from another side of the triangle. One problem with this approach is that, given the imbalance in Asian–American trade flows, almost any move towards Europe can be viewed by Washington as a direct challenge. Several strong Asian economies have already diversified their financial and monetary holdings, and have understood the necessity of dialogue with European countries to broaden their business activities without too many obstacles. But in some areas, where European firms are relatively strong and Asia is globally dependent on the United States, any move seems to imply political consequences. This is particularly true of the aerospace industry, an area in which Europe now faces enormous problems, but where it has much to offer the market. Can East Asia's leading economies claim a free-trade policy and open entry into the EC when they are still tied almost exclusively to US firms as a supplier or a partner in this area? American lobbying has been very effective in this regard, helping to lessen trade pressures thanks to Asian priority procurement of advanced technologies in America. And most firms may have lacked the commercial aggressiveness and presence of their American counterparts in the past. But it will be very hard to explain to the European public why the external trade borders of the Community should be wide open if leading European products are not marketed in Asia. In some cases Europe can provide technologies previously unavailable in Asian countries. For example, the French satellite Spot has been available since the beginning of 1992, with a special software interpretation programme to map poppy-field cultivation in the 'Golden Triangle' of Thailand,[6] and there are now decisions pending on many Asian satellites.[7]

These are only examples. Cooperation in some of these key sectors could be developed. Foreign financial partnership with such new actors as Singapore Aerospace, Taiwan Aerospace, Japanese, Korean and other manufacturers, should not be restricted to American firms. This requires a degree of forward planning by European industry. To map out these possibilities in detail clearly goes beyond the scope of this paper.

But the idea itself could be thrown open for discussion: nearly exclusive Asian ties, in the areas of high technology, with the United States, are a product of post-Second World War history. After the end of the Cold War, these links can now be made more diverse: this does not necessarily imply questioning the primacy of the US security connection with Asia. And conversely, for the same historical reasons, European markets in the past 40 years have been on the whole less receptive to Asian products than the American market. Europe is the single largest economic region in the world. It is actively seeking investment from the most developed economies of Asia, in part to help diminish its trade imbalance in consumer goods. But if Asia's economic powers want to secure a relatively controversy-free access to this market, they should think of tapping these high-technology resources and participating in their growth. This is already useful for the future of mutual relations, even before the Community itself builds up to the point at which it can pursue an active external strategy in this area.

Europe's strategic and political relations with Asia, and especially with East Asia, are in a different category altogether than the United States' historical relationship with these countries. Any talk of a 'triangle' can only be speculation about a future trade war between regional blocs, and this does not accord with the present trend towards growing global trade. Furthermore, the end of the Cold War opens up the possibility of undifferentiated relations between regions and countries, with less political dialogue between regions: in this respect, the US approach to security could encourage these developments. Indeed, it is in the interests of both Asia and Europe not to counteract this trend which has offered genuine guarantees in the recent past. Indeed, they should complement it in a multilateral spirit, defusing in the process the misunderstandings that can occur in the arena of global trade.

Notes

[1] The total figure for Asia, excluding Cambodia, is around $210m. This should be seen in the light of the $18 billion that the EC has committed to Africa in the last round of the Lomé convention.

[2] These figures are summarized from a study by Philippe Lasserre and Charlotte Butler, 'The European Presence in Asia: Problems and Prospects', *Euro-Asia Centre News*, no. 23, INSEAD, Fontainebleau.

[3] See François Godement (ed.), *Le désarmement nucléaire en Asie, L'autre volet de l'accord FNI* (Paris: Masson, 1990).

[4] Giulio Andreotti's remarks included the idea that the EC permanent seat would replace that of Britain and France, which was perhaps greeted with less enthusiasm on the other side of the Alps. See *Le Monde*, 19 September 1990.

[5] *Ibid.*, 5 August 1992.

[6] *AFP Sciences,* news dispatch no. 792, 24 October 1991, p. 16.

[7] TCS, *La Lettre des Satellites*, no. 71, 15 May 1992.

What Role for Europe in Asian Affairs?

FUMIAKI TAKAHASHI

After the Second World War, Europe withdrew militarily from Asia.[1] In the political field as well, Europe's role in Asia has decreased and its political interest has waned, due partly to the presence there of the United States, which has taken the greatest responsibility for the region's security, and partly to the influence of the former USSR and China during the Cold War. In the economic field, however, Europe has remained interested in the region and, in spite of – perhaps even because of – progress in the economic integration of the European Community (EC) and the economic development of East Asian countries, has contributed to the region's prosperity.

East Asia now has the world's fastest-growing economy, and a dynamic one, and has become a region which can assert influence, at least in the economic field, on a global scale. This coincides with the end of the Cold War and the collapse of the Soviet Union which have affected international relationships in Asia, although not as dramatically as in Europe. But as this new situation is bound to bring about a fundamental change in the structure of international politics, this in turn will gradually induce new developments in the international situation in East Asia. In this context, how will the relationship between Europe and Asia develop from now onwards?

East Asia and western Europe: the present situation
East Asia is not only made up of countries with very varied geopolitical characteristics – including population size, geographical factors, political and social systems, the degree of economic development and military capability – but also the peoples themselves vary greatly in their ethnic, linguistic, religious, traditional and other cultural aspects. Given both the different colonial pasts of the European countries and their current interest in the region, the roles they play there vary accordingly. Thus generalizations about the relationship between the two continents are hard to make.

ECONOMY
As a result of global economic growth in recent years, the economic ties between Europe and Asia, which generate 30% and 20% of world national income respectively, have steadily strengthened. East Asia is a region in which the countries' economic size and stage of development, together with their economic structures and systems, differ enormously. The degree of importance which Europe has attached to its

relations with these countries is roughly proportional to the degree of economic activity of the particular country or group of countries. Thus Europe's most significant relationship is with Japan, the only industrialized democracy in the region, accounting for 70% of its economy. The other countries in the region are basically developing countries and, among them, Europe has important relations with those Asian newly industrialized economies (ANIEs) which are about to join the ranks of the industrialized countries, followed by the Association of South-East Asian Nations (ASEAN) countries which are promoting industrialization and pursuing the ANIEs. Europe's economic relations with China are no less impressive than its relations with the ASEAN countries, although its ties with Indochina and other non-ASEAN states are not yet as close.

The EC has recently and rapidly increased its trade with East Asia; the annual average increase in exports from 1986 to 1990 was 14%, and for imports it was 16%. This surpassed the growth rate of Europe's world trade in the same period. On the other hand, Europe's trade balance *vis-à-vis* Asia shows a deficit of approximately 10 billion ECU, even excluding Japan. Investment has also recently become more active, and the percentage of investment between the two regions over total world direct investment reached 6% in 1990. European private funds are contributing to the growth of developing countries in East Asia, although the amount of European investment in the region is smaller than that between North America and East Asia and that within East Asia. Also, the accumulated amount of European investment in Japan remains only 10% of Japanese investment in Europe over the past 40 years. European countries also extend financial assistance to low-income countries and technological assistance to East Asia, although its priority is higher in other regions.

Thus western European countries have participated in economic activity in East Asia and, while they have benefited from it through increased exports and other means, they have also contributed to the region's growing economic prosperity. Because of the many developing countries in East Asia, Europe's contribution to economic development also implies a contribution to the region's political stability. The recent remarkable economic performance of the ANIEs and the ASEAN countries has made their trade structure *vis-à-vis* Europe similar to that between industrialized countries. For example, 64% of ASEAN exports to the EC in 1988 were manufactured products. Electrical machinery, as well as textiles and clothing, are showing rapid growth replacing the traditional export of primary goods. Europe, through importing manufactured products from ASEAN and the ANIEs, can thus play a role in promoting their industrialization. Trade frictions between the two regions are likely to gain in importance, but such problems should be resolved by making adjustments both to the industrial structures of the developed countries, and within the framework of the General Agreement on Tariffs and Trade (GATT).

The EC's intraregional trade as a percentage of its world trade increased from 50% in 1980 to 60% in 1991. Intraregional trade in East Asia, however, remains only 30% of the total as of 1990, and East Asia depends greatly upon extraregional trade, including with Europe whose role is relatively small. The economic realities of East Asia may be grasped more adequately by placing it in the broader context of the Asia–Pacific region as a whole, which extends to North America and Australia. The role of the US market and capital is significant in that it supports high growth in Asia, and Japan and the United States still play a leading role in the region's trade and investment with Europe's contributions following them. Some countries in the region hope for a third competitor to alleviate their dependence upon Japan and the US, and there are those whose trade or investment *vis-à-vis* the EC is actually larger than *vis-à-vis* the US.

On the other hand, the relative importance for European countries of economic links with East Asia in relation to their global economic relationship is not so large. For instance, in 1991, the percentage of trade with Japan remained 3.2% and with ASEAN 1.6%. This would seem to be due to the fact that, in Europe, intraregional exchanges in the highly homogeneous economic space can yield profits quickly, and also that the EC countries have concentrated on promoting economic integration to strengthen their industry and economy. In contrast, the percentage of trade with the EC for Asian countries is generally large at around 10–20%.

SECURITY

Security in Asia is guaranteed by the United States through its bilateral arrangements with Japan, Korea, the Philippines and other countries in the region, and through the forward deployment of its military forces. In the first half of the Cold War era, Europe gradually reduced its military presence in Asia and now only the UK, which has traditionally been interested in this region, stations modest forces in Hong Kong and Brunei. The UK, through the Five Power Defence Agreement (FPDA), also plays a role in the defence of Singapore and Malaysia. There are several reasons why Europe, despite its own economic and other interests in the region, has placed the military role in this region of high strategic importance in the Cold War era in the hands of the United States.

First, East Asia is geographically far from Europe. Conventional forces on a scale large enough to meet the security requirements of the region would be immensely expensive to deploy, and far in excess of the capabilities of western European countries. Moreover, in North-east Asia – strategically the most important subregion and where the former Soviet Union and China, both nuclear powers, have had significant interests – the extension of nuclear deterrence has been indispensable. Second, as the colonies gained independence, the economic interests of the former European colonial powers diminished. Instead, it gradually became evident that, under the free trading system, substantial economic benefits could be gained in the region without the added weight of armed forces; indeed, the cost-effectiveness of military power has declined. Third, in terms of the degree of interest in East Asia, there has been a discrepancy between that of former suzerain states or major powers such as the UK, France and Germany, and that of other states. Fourth, the importance of the United States' presence, whose power has been something to be trusted in the eyes of Asian countries, cannot be underestimated. Fifth, the security interests of western Europe have been directed solely at dealing with the Soviet threat, in cooperation with the United States, on the European front.

While its security ties with East Asia are extremely weak, Europe has had important, if not vital, interests in this region, even if these have not always been recognized. First, it enjoyed the economic benefits summarized above. Second, as economic relationships are based on political stability, Europe was as interested in the domestic stability of East Asian countries based on a market economy system as it was in the overall peace and stability of the region. Third, should the former Soviet Union or 'World Communism' have succeeded in large-scale expansion in East Asia, given the region's economic vitality, the power balance would have tilted towards the Soviet Union, thus increasing the Soviet threat on the European front. This in turn could have meant the diversion to the Asian front of US military resources allocated to Europe, and the possibility of war as a result of the extreme tension between the superpowers. These are the scenarios which Europe has wanted to avoid more than anything else. Fourth, preventing isolationism from gathering strength in the United States has been indispensable for European defence. If the US were to reduce its commitment in East Asia due to indifference on the part of its allies, it would have unfavourable effects on the European front as well. On the other hand, such interests have probably not been recognized to the full extent. For instance, Europe was critical of US intervention in Vietnam for fear that this would jeopardize the North Atlantic Treaty Organization's ability to cope with the Soviet threat in Europe.

POLITICS
Although Europe's military presence in the region has been very limited, in the latter half of the Cold War era it has been showing some interest in the security of Asia as well as in the closely related regional and international political issues. And in many instances Europe has taken a common stand with the United States and Japan. A symbolic example of this is the US–Soviet intermediate-range nuclear forces (INF) negotiations. Japan, the US and Europe acknowledged the indivisibility of security and, as a result of these negotiations, succeeded in realizing a common position, recognizing that a situation which had temporarily improved the level of security in Europe – but at the same time adversely affected Asia – would in time have threatened European security. A common position, however, has not been reached easily. It is natural for countries to give greater priority to attainable

aims nearer home rather than to situations in far-away regions. Moreover, in cases where the degree of interest is relatively low – for example, the Korean peninsula for Europe and the former Yugoslavia for Asia – the perception of whether an incident has global implications or not is less acute when viewed from outside the region concerned. For Europe, the East Asian region is a lower priority on its diplomatic agenda. In addition to its concern over European integration and its relations *vis-à-vis* the US, the EC is also currently devoting itself to its relations with eastern Europe and the former Soviet Union. Furthermore, Europe also has to look after its political interests in the Middle East, the Maghreb and Africa. In the past six years, the heads of state and foreign ministers of the Group of Seven (G-7) countries in Europe only visited Japan for political consultation once or twice each. The German Chancellor and the French President had not made any such visits in this period.

The relative weakness in the Euro-Asian political relationship, as compared to the economic one, is not without its reasons. First, just as Europe cannot provide Asia with security commitments, Asia is no more equipped for such provision *vis-à-vis* Europe. Second, Asia is neither sufficiently politically organized, lacking as it does in cohesiveness, nor in a position to speak with one voice with global influence. Third, in a situation in which the importance of Asia for European security is limited – and for the European economy relatively limited – Europe's sense of political solidarity towards those Asian countries which are perceived as economic 'threats' tends to be slight. Fourth, East Asia – apart from Japan – is basically a developing area, and its relationship with Europe over issues of international politics and economics has involved a conflict of interests between industrialized nations and non-aligned nations and, in some cases, emotional confrontations between an ex-suzerain state and an ex-colony. Moreover, socialist states contribute factors that complicate interests even in relations between western European states and free nations in East Asia when dealing with regional issues. Finally, partly due to their intensive exchanges in all fields with the US and Japan, the East Asian countries' interest in and understanding of western Europe is less than they exhibit towards the US and Japan. Their language, religion and culture are substantially different from those of Europe, and they tend to react against European experience and values when these are proposed as absolutes.

In spite of the above constraints, in recent years European countries have been supportive of the efforts of free nations in Asia in dealing with their international political problems. This reflects the expanding basis of interest shared by European and Asian countries. To cite some examples, European countries have been actively supporting South Korea's position in the international arena over the issue of North–South unification, its UN membership and North Korea's suspected nuclear development. The refugee problem in Indochina is an issue relevant to the stability of ASEAN and other neighbouring countries, as well as to the stability of the entire region, and western European countries have contributed by accepting refugees and providing assistance to the asylum countries. As for the Cambodian problem, France and some other European countries have been playing their part in its solution in cooperation with Indonesia and other countries in the region. Contributions have also been made by the Europeans in support of the Philippines, assistance for the democratization of Mongolia and support for regional efforts to fight against the drugs trade. On the other hand, when dealing with political issues involving cultural differences and antagonism against former suzerain states, rather than concern with common interests such as security and economic aspects, confrontation can occur. Human rights problems and environmental issues are typical cases in point. In contrast, seen from the European side, when political systems differ, even when certain economic ties exist, confrontation over political problems can easily spill over into the economic arena. Europe has traditionally deemed China more important than Japan as a large potential market and as a politically influential country. However, as was recently seen in the Tiananmen Square incident, political aspects – including human rights – can cool political relationships and shrink economic ties.

Euro-Japanese relations and Japan–US relations

Throughout the post-war era, the relationship with the United States has been the top priority for both Japan and Europe, their mutual relationship being limited to the economic field for a long time. When dealing with occasional economic frictions, the incentive for compromise has been relatively weak, while the limited nature of the overall relationship has proved beneficial in resolving problems according to economic logic, free from political considerations. Therefore, while Japan entertained the feeling that the EC applied discriminatory protectionist measures towards it on the one hand, the EC could easily have felt that Japan made concessions only to the US and shifted the strain to the EC. The EC tends particularly to feel that because Japan entrusts its security to the US, it yields to the US on economic markets, which is incorrect. As Japan's trade with the US is 1.6 times as large as that with the EC, and investment 2.4 times as large, Japan's relationship with the United States, even only in economic aspects, is so important that it cannot be replaced by that with the EC. (The Euro-American relationship is even closer; trade is double and investment is seven times as large as in the Euro-Japanese case.) It should also be noted that the concessions Japan makes to the US are automatically applied to the EC as well. On the other hand, the necessity for adjustments in economic relations tends to rise in proportion to the closeness of the bilateral relationship in general.

The EC does not have the close consultation and cooperation on international political problems with Japan as Japan does with the US. It is only in the past few years that western Europe has developed an interest in the political role of Japan, a member of the G-7, after Japan established its economic strength. The turmoil in Europe after 1989 has also contributed to this. It is not too much to say that until then how to cope with Japan's 'aggressive economic behaviour' was at the centre of the EC's approach to its relationship with Japan. It was as recently as July 1991 that the Japan–EC joint declaration giving priority to political relations was announced.

Japan may, at times, have been more or less neglectful of its political relations with Europe, but it played an important role in extending economic assistance to Turkey, a wing of NATO, in the 1980s, and recently, it has come to pay due consideration to European contributions to global security. For example, Japan provided the UK and France with a portion of the $11.4bn financial contribution to the coalition forces against Iraq during the Gulf War – although the bulk of this was designated to the US forces. The recent decision to establish a special relationship between the Conference on Security and Cooperation in Europe (CSCE) and Japan indicates recognition of the necessity to initiate greater cooperation on both sides.

As the Japan–US relationship gradually moves closer to that of the US and Europe, both countries should be able to solve peacefully those economic frictions which are bound to arise from time to time, and this should not adversely affect the Euro-Japanese relationship. Even so, it is still desirable as far as is possible to solve problems in multilateral frameworks in the post-Cold War era when trilateral coordination has become increasingly important. Thus the interests of Japan, the US and Europe should be balanced as much as possible and Japan and Europe must make conscious efforts in that direction.

East Asia after the Cold War
Examining the characteristics of the security environment in East Asia and how the end of the Cold War might change them provides a clue to how international relations in the region might turn out in the post-Cold War era.

First, since most countries in the region are developing countries, their policy priorities have been directed towards economic development rather than reducing military tension, and this tendency will continue with the end of the Cold War. The current trend towards a market economy in the socialist countries in Asia will flow into the main stream of East Asian economic development.

Second, there are a number of factors within the region, including the issue of China, which do not fall into a clear-cut East–West dichotomy. Thus, the effect of the end of East–West confrontation on the enhancement of stability has been attenuated to a certain extent. The China factor still remains; Russian power is declining; the importance of the ANIEs is growing; and the process of multipolarization should progress. How to integrate Russia into the region has emerged as an important new question.

Third, in this region, the conflict of interests among nations is complex and their threat perceptions are diverse, thus making the overall security configuration extremely complicated. The sources of conflict created by the former Soviet Union's support of socialist states are no longer there now that Russia is aiming towards democratic status. On the other hand, the framework of the East–West relationship, which used to perform a certain function in preventing the occurrence or expansion of regional conflicts, is no longer available. This is relevant in cases where conflicts of interest between countries in the region become acute before their economic standards rise to the level at which there would be less incentive to resort to military means. It would therefore be wise to prepare for the probability of new regional conflicts occurring.

Fourth, among the unresolved disputes and conflicts which exist in the region, the Cambodian conflict is in its last stage of resolution as a result of the end of the Cold War. This has also had a favourable effect on the North–South confrontation in the Korean peninsula, but it is still uncertain whether or not North Korea will open up to the outside world. The Northern Territorial issue between Japan and Russia has not progressed towards a solution because Russia, influenced by the military and by nationalism, has not yet changed its Cold War attitude towards Asia. Only after resolving these issues can the calamity brought about by communism in Asia be fully eradicated.

Finally, this region has been pursuing economic interdependency based on political, social and cultural diversity among countries, while a move towards integration as seen in Europe has not been felt. The end of the Cold War seems unlikely to influence this fact immediately. There may be emerging movements that call for the organization of economic and political cooperation, but they are likely to be caused by factors inherent in this region, such as the requirements resulting from economic development and the necessity of adjusting various conflicts of interest.

In sum, the effects of the end of the Cold War and the collapse of the Soviet Union are less significant in Asia than in Europe. This implies two things: first, the tendency for economic logic to work free from political considerations was and is relatively strong in Asia; and second, the Soviet factor has been less important for the security of Asia as a whole, North-east Asia excepted, than it was in Europe.

RUSSIA
The enormous military build-up in the far east of the former Soviet Union has had a marginal effect on Asia as a whole due to geostrategical factors. The former Soviet Union failed to translate this into political influence because of the US military counterbalance in the region. This, however, is not to deny that the Soviet military threat has been perceived as serious by its neighbouring countries. Although the emergence of Russia after the Cold War reduced the military threat, this has again had a less dramatic impact in Asia than in Europe. The disappearance of the Warsaw Treaty Organisation (WTO), the Soviet military withdrawal from Germany and eastern Europe, the

emergence of a buffer zone comprising the three Baltic States, Ukraine and Byelarus in addition to eastern Europe, have all dramatically changed the geopolitical situation in Europe. Russia and its forces have receded far from the western European horizon and the lead-time for Russia to attack western Europe has increased greatly; it now seems almost impossible for Russia to win back eastern Europe. Nothing of the sort has taken place in North-east Asia. The Russian border and its forces have not receded an inch with the end of the Cold War. If more advanced military resources were to be deployed in the Far East because of their withdrawal from the European front, and if greater priority were given to the Far-East fleets because of constraints in the Baltics and the Black Sea, this would reverse the trend towards improving the situation. Also, Russia is trying to identify itself with western Europe culturally as well as politically, and therefore has been identifying less with Asia. Russia, as a Eurasian state, claims to be a bridge from Europe to Asia, but its foreign policy towards Asia has a low priority. Moreover, in the Far East, the military–industrial complex has a firm basis and remains conservative. If NATO now considers Russian instability and uncertainty a risk, it is not surprising that Asia should also be vigilant to the movements of far-eastern Russia, even by European standards. Furthermore, if one accepts that the reconstruction of an economy or of a military organization is far easier than the alteration of geopolitical realities, anxieties concerning Russia are far stronger in North-east Asia, where Russia maintains an enormous military capability that can be deployed, than they are in Europe. It is legitimate for Europe to wish for a democratic system to take root as soon as possible in Russia, and the West should do all it can to support this. And yet Europe must also remember that Russia has another face when seen from North-east Asia, as mentioned above, and that this has global implications.

If Russia wants to play its role in Asia as a country that shares common values with the West, it should first of all accept the West's position advocating the liquidation of Russia's Stalinist and Cold War heritage, and swiftly reduce its military forces which far surpass its requirements for self-defence in the Far East. Through such moves, Russia's policy stance would move closer to that of the West, as has already been demonstrated in the Korean peninsula and Cambodia; and a way for Russia to participate in the economic development of East Asia would be opened. Russia, when it participates in consultations over Asian issues, should respect the ways of Asia and refrain from introducing new destabilizing factors in its security environment through such acts as the export of weapons. Western European countries can put pressure on Russia to adopt policies that take into consideration the wishes of Asian countries. They can also avoid advocating that Asia should emulate the European framework of regional security after the Cold War by understanding the characteristics of the Asian security environment.

CHANGES IN THE WESTERN EUROPE–EAST ASIAN RELATIONSHIP
Will the end of the Cold War and the collapse of the Soviet Union
change the conditions that prescribed the role of western Europe in
East Asian affairs? If so, what might these changes be? The factors
governing why Europe played so small a military role in Asia must
now be examined. First, the limitation in Europe's capabilities, which
is the most important point, is unlikely to change in the near future, and
the effectiveness of military power will continue to decline. As to the
presence of US forces, though some worry about their withdrawal, the
author believes that, essentially, its forward deployment will be maintained. The discrepancies among European countries' interests in the
region will diminish due to the progress in EC political integration and
deepening interdependency in the post-Cold War era. Europe can also
decrease its resource allocation for coping with uncertain security
factors arising from the former Soviet Union. New developments are
taking place in Europe which are forcing it to devote itself to European
affairs, but these can be resolved in the long run.

As regards any change in European interests in East Asia, its economic interests should increase further as long as the free trading
system and regional stability are maintained. Should confrontation
over economic interests become acute and either of the parties take to
protectionism, or should the common recognition of or shared interests
in security be lost, the interest in political stability could also disappear. In the former case, an adjustment of interests would take place
before such a stage were reached. As for the latter, the concept of the
indivisibility of security that stood between Europe and East Asia via
the Soviet (Russian) threat seems to have disappeared. On the other
hand, it is unlikely that Europe's political interests, detached from its
economic relations, are going to grow in East Asia. Therefore there is a
risk that, unless the recognition of a common security interest is
confirmed from a different perspective, the relationship between the
two regions may either worsen or become remote. Europe can indi-
rectly contribute to East Asian stability by keeping US forces in
Europe thereby preventing the US from becoming isolationist. In sum,
any increase in the interests of Europe in East Asia seems unlikely to
go so far as to justify changes in the basic European policy concerning
its security role in Asia.

Asia's political influence could increase in the long term, depending upon the degree of economic development and progress in regional
cooperation in East Asia, which would help attenuate confrontational
attitudes between industrialized and developing countries in Europe
and Asia. But when shared security interests decrease, perceptions of
political solidarity decrease even further. Besides, the cultural differences between the two regions are basically irrelevant to the Cold War,
and should be overcome through unremitting efforts for mutual understanding by both regions. In total, as far as Asia is concerned, the end
of the Cold War is unlikely to create new obstacles to the efforts made

by both regions towards intensifying their political relations. On the other hand, there is a risk that Europe, which should have been endowed with a global view, may further concentrate purely on European affairs. Asian countries generally expect western Europe to play a role in neutralizing the influence of the US and Japan, and Japan also welcomes any European role that reassures its Asian partners. Thus, a western Europe interested in Asia serves the best interests of the region.

Interdependency and 'mutual engagement'

The collapse of the Soviet communist regime occurred because of its inability to adapt to the transnationalization of economic activities, progress in science and technology, and the evolution of an information society, all of which are contrary to the nature of a regime which suppresses individual initiatives and survives only in a closed society. This tide is, at the same time, rising and deepening interdependency among countries, and economic development in East Asia in recent years has been achieved by riding on this tide which is thus changing the component factors of power in international relations. These changes, in turn, are inducing a realignment of power relations among states. Thus, in the post-Cold War world, power is becoming dispersed, creating a multipolar structure in which each pole depends on the other. World peace and prosperity, therefore, cannot be secured without coordination and cooperation among major countries which share common objectives and values. This means that the bases on which the US, Europe and Japan share common interests and aims not only in the economic, but also in the security and political areas are expanding. It is therefore inaccurate to claim that the removal of the Soviet threat will lead to a worsening relationship among these three regional players as a result of bilateral economic frictions. On the other hand, as the new structure is multipolar and fragile, the participation of major countries in solving important transnational issues is even more necessary, and conscious efforts need to be made to achieve common goals. One such is the need to increase the intensity of consultations between Europe on the one hand, and Japan and other East Asian countries on the other. Creating new fora for this purpose is unrealistic for the time being, thus bilateral consultations and multilateral cooperation within existing frameworks, such as the ASEAN Post-Ministerial Conference (PMC), should be increased. Such issues as the improvement of the peacekeeping and conflict-prevention functions of the UN, nuclear non-proliferation, discipline in the export of weapons, human rights and the environment could be the subject of such a course of action. Furthermore, it is important to strengthen the G-7 – the forum for the trilateral cooperation among Japan, US and Europe – as a place not only for economic, but also for political consultation.

This growing interdependency is compatible neither with exclusive regionalism nor with regional blocs. It cannot be denied that recently, not only in the economic, but also in the political field, the concerns of each region were divided in such a way that the EC was interested in Europe and the former Soviet Union (as well as in the Middle East and Africa at times), the US was interested in the American continents, and Japan was interested in the Asia–Pacific region. The major countries should, while refraining from the temptation to establish spheres of influence, consciously endeavour both to promote cooperation with outside regions, and to engage in matters of important concern to different regions. This, in turn, would contribute to upgrading the recognition of shared benefits and responsibilities among different regions. Japan has recently been increasing its international responsibilities by deepening its relationship with Europe, including its association with the CSCE, and, furthermore, by participating in support for eastern Europe (G24), support for the former Soviet Union (the Washington Process and others) and the multilateral conference for peace in the Middle East. Japan's bilateral official development assistance (ODA) to Africa has increased from 6.3% of the total ODA in 1977 to 15.3% in 1989. Europe, for its part, is expected not only to continue with its engagement in East Asia, but also to strengthen it. Today, Europe holds three of the permanent five (Perm 5), four of the G-7 and two-thirds of the Organisation for Economic Cooperation and Development (OECD) seats, and thus enjoys a large representation, making its global responsibility accordingly large. By the same token, just as European countries participate in the United Nations Transitional Authority in Cambodia (UNTAC), Japan should also be seeking to participate in the peacekeeping operations in Yugoslavia and elsewhere where European interests are at stake. APEC should accelerate its work to consolidate its aims and methods of organization and cooperation, and thereby forms of engagement with Europe should appear on its agenda as soon as possible. East Asian countries that promote global cooperation with Europe are no longer limited to Japan; Korea is hoping to join the OECD in a short while. Along with progress in economic development in East Asia, the foundations and scope of cooperation between Europe and East Asia should expand further. Now it is time to start discussing how to expand mutual engagement between the two regions.

Notes

[1] In this paper, 'Europe' is understood as western Europe, comprised mainly of European Community and European Free Trade Association (EFTA) countries, unless stated otherwise. In view of the present diversified relationship between European countries and East Asia, Europe is sometimes represented by certain major countries such as the UK, France or Germany in the context of its relations with specific Asian countries or subregions. East Asia, comprising North-east and South-east Asia, includes Japan, the Korean peninsula, China, the Association of South-East Asian Nations (ASEAN) countries, Indochina and Myanmar; and far-eastern Russia is also taken into account. The Indian subcontinent is not discussed here.

Conclusion

FRANÇOIS HEISBOURG

Over the past few years, massive strategic change has occurred in Europe and the former Soviet Union, and the Cold War's grip has weakened: no more Iron Curtain, no more Berlin Wall, no more divided Germany; indeed, no more USSR – the last of the great pre-First World War autocracies has finally met an end delayed by 70 years of communism, and history has resumed its march. On the other hand, things look very different from the Asian perspective. The Cold War has maintained its hold only a few miles to the north of Seoul, and there still exists an 'arc of Asian socialism' to use Dr Chung-min Lee's expression. The current pace of change in East Asia is clearly different to the breakneck speed which continues to remodel Europe and the former USSR. Furthermore, strategic changes in Asia are likely to manifest themselves in rather different ways to those occurring in the West. In addition, defining future strategic roles in Asia will depend on domestic factors at least as much, and generally more, than on external pressures. In this context, our conference posed several basic questions which underlay the specific issues addressed at various stages of the proceedings:

- To what extent (and with what effects) will a basic transformation of the strategic landscape occur in East Asia, both *sui generis* and as a result of the collapse of Soviet rule and the end of the Cold War?
- To what degree will an international system emerge in Asia which will not be simply a function of conflicts or alignments defined elsewhere? Indeed this question, which was at the heart of Sir Michael Howard's presentation, can also be put in an Asia-centric mode: to what degree will the future world system be shaped by the new Asian strategic order?
- Over the next few years, how will change in East Asia be managed? Can a transition as benign as the one in western Europe in 1989–91 be expected (although it remains to be seen whether the ease of that transformation was not a curse in disguise as multiple conflicts threaten Europe's post-communist societies)? Will the management of change imply more assertive national policies, or greater reliance on multilateral institutions?
- What role will the major countries involved in the region play in the future: a United States with an increasingly domestic agenda; a Japan in search of its place in the international system; a China on the eve of succession; a Korean peninsula faced with the prospect of reunification; a troubled Indian subcontinent; and a Russia in the throes of revolutionary change?

In discussing these and other issues, we were fortunate to have a number of Russian and Kazakh participants; conversely, the conference suffered from a dearth of South-east Asian participants (due to a meeting involving a number of them in Bangkok) and the non-participation of our members living in the People's Republic of China.

In examining the prospects for change in the region, Prime Minister Chung Won-shik indicated that it was his government's wish that the reunification of the two Koreas be realized by the end of this decade.

He also emphasized two points which re-emerged in various guises in our proceedings. First, that 'bitterness and regret caused by aggression and annexation committed in the era of colonialism are still not dispelled and remain a source of distrust'. He mentioned no country in particular, but the meaning was clear enough: as was pointed out in the debate in Plenary I and in Committee, future security also implies a need to come to terms with the past. Secondly, he noted the Asian–Pacific 'mission to take the lead to a world economy based on the open global trading order, thereby countering any trend towards protectionist regionalism in the other parts of the world'. Here again, the code was not difficult to break, and Plenary II subsequently gave us the opportunity to underscore the strategic implications of trade and financial issues in the post-Cold War era.

Plenary I
Professor Sir Michael Howard, in his thought-provoking analysis 'Old Conflicts and New Disorders', made the essential point that the Asian countries may have inherited old conflicts from the West, but any new disorders will be their own. In effect, international politics in the Pacific and East Asia are no longer a subsystem of those in the West, most recently of the Cold War confrontation; Sir Michael cogently stressed the role of the United States, whose presence is 'one reason why the Pacific remains pacific'. Two comments made by Sir Michael were of particular interest. First, that modernization is an export of the West, and thus an external challenge to societies faced with the difficulties of incredibly rapid adaptation. Furthermore, no society in or outside Asia is invulnerable to politically extreme approaches to modernization. And second, that democracies can be belligerent, and too much faith should not be placed in the argument that they do not fight each other.

In his response, Yukio Satoh chided Sir Michael for using the Eurocentric expression 'the Far East'. In stressing the stabilizing role of the US in the region he noted that an adequate level of Japanese defence spending helped generate support in the US for maintaining the presence of its forces. However, he noted that there was no single dominant power in East Asia, not even the United States; this creates a very different situation from the one which generated Europe's security institutions during the Cold War. Hence, if multilateral security dialogues evolved in Asia, they would be of a different nature to those in

Europe. Scepticism was expressed from the floor about 'dialogue for dialogue's sake', which one participant called 'political escapism'. Although European-style confidence-building measures may be applicable to the Korean peninsula, the speakers from the floor generally agreed with Yukio Satoh that European-style multilateralism was not to be expected. Indeed, given the apparent incapacity of European institutions to cope with violence in post-communist Europe itself, these doubts are bound to be shared.

There was also substantial discussion about the relationship between financial assistance and political stability: it was stated that providing money tends to generate greater stability only if a modicum of stability already exists (as was the case with the Marshall Plan). Nonetheless, Japan's tight-fisted policy towards Russia drew a fair amount of criticism from the floor, notably on the grounds of Japan's individualistic handling of the Northern Territories issue; these comments heralded the proceedings of Committee 2 on Japan's search for a normal role: if the lack of Japanese leadership creates concern, would greater Japanese assertiveness be any less controversial?

Plenary II
Professor Stuart Harris faced the daunting task of bringing together economic issues and security affairs in his paper 'The Economic Aspects of Pacific Security'. For although there is much glib talk about the need to emphasize the economic factors of security and to conceptualize the relationship between economics and security, this is much easier said than done. Stuart's examination of the interactions between economic growth, trade links, socio-economic disparities, interdependence and international security is a model of the genre. His contention that uncertainty is now the only certain element drew no rebuttal; and his point, raised anew in the ensuing debate, that interdependence, contrary to conventional wisdom, can increase conflict when states fear each other is an important one. However, his emphasis on the need to integrate economic factors and security issues in multilateral dialogue – notably in the Association of South-East Asian Nations (ASEAN) – did not go without comment.

Dr Peter Ackerman posited the increasing difficulty of integrating economic and security issues for the following reasons. The timeframes involved are generally not the same, making it difficult to use economic instruments to reach a given national security result. (In the debate, the point was made that the pace of evolution between economics and security is not necessarily of a different order: simply, the cycles of evolution rarely coincide, be they short term or long term in nature.) Economic trends are usually self-correcting, whereas security trends are not. Hostile economic actions, short of acts of war, are losing their sting and are therefore less amenable to manipulation for national security purposes. Political leaders have less (and decreasing) control of economic realities than they have of security policies; indeed, defining the national economic self-interest has become increasingly awkward as a result of complex interdependence.

Conversely, Ackerman noted that interdependent economic structures can be highly vulnerable to the threat of violence, notably by non-state actors: the impact of terrorist threats during the Gulf War on international travel and related activities may have been a taste of things to come.

In the debate, the question of China's economic growth and its impact on security policy was repeatedly raised, an issue which mobilized the energies of Committee 1.

Committee 1

In Committee 1, 'China: Between Ideology and Interdependence', there was an archetypal demonstration of the extent to which domestic factors influence the redefinition of security policies and roles in East and South Asia.

Professor Yasheng Huang's basic thesis was that China's security interests are increasingly being defined economically. Thus China would hardly be tempted by a re-run of its 1962 and 1979-style confrontations with India and Vietnam; whereas the Spratly Islands offer a real possibility for armed conflict since economic interests are perceived as being at stake. Harry Harding took a less sanguine line than Huang on the overriding dynamic of economic growth, which in the latter's view was largely independent of political vicissitudes. Harding argued that the absence of political reform could lead to decay (including economic decay) as unbridled centrifugal forces take their toll and the legitimacy of the central government is eroded. Indeed, in the debate some participants, albeit a small minority, argued that debilitating influences of this kind had already progressed to the degree that cataclysmic breakdown could occur at some point.

In discussing China between the Yang of the Maoist legacy and the Yin of modernization, all speakers felt that a return to the totalitarian model could be ruled out, and that continued reform was inevitable.

The discussion of issues such as uneven development, dissidence, the attitudes of the central elite versus the regional elite (*vis-à-vis* the desirability of further reforms) revealed a variety of perceptions, but little to contradict the general assessment that the next phase will most likely be that of 'neo-authoritarianism' or an attempt to follow the so-called 'Asian path'. A stable, long-term authoritarian solution is not likely, however: either it would lead to a more basically altered, relatively efficacious new economic and political order; or to a protracted decline. Most participants seemed to opt for the former, but there was no real attempt to ascertain which of many possible forms an eventually 'fully reformed' China would be most likely to manifest.

The second main topic discussed in Committee 1 concerned the security implications of these developments for China's neighbours. It was agreed that a very significant growth in Chinese military strength is perhaps inevitable and natural (if in a sense paradoxical, given the sudden absence of powerful adversaries). The region may simply have to learn to live with an increasingly powerful China, but its members should make clear that they expect cooperative behaviour and a constructive approach to problem-solving, or else they, including Japan, may band together or seek support elsewhere to counterbalance Chinese power.

Speakers pointed to the virtual certainty of an increase in assertive nationalism on the part of Chinese leaders. There was nervous talk of Chinese irredentist tendencies and of a hegemonic 'Middle Kingdom' syndrome. Furthermore, it was pointed out that China's perceptions of where its vital interests lie would, as always, tend to expand in step with added power. By and large there was a consensus that involving China in regional affairs was all to the good, but only on condition that the Chinese be made to accept, and eventually to internalize, the obligations – in terms of self-restraint and responsible adherence to the modern rules of the international game – of interdependence.

It is worth noting that no discussion of energy, population, environmental limits and so on took place throughout the Committee's deliberation, not withstanding their security implications.

Committee 2
In analysing 'Japan in Search of a Normal Role', Professor Takashi Inoguchi made the interesting point that maybe Japan was less 'abnormal' than the question assumed, and that the United States may instead be the 'abnormal' power in the post-Cold War world; in effect, Inoguchi posited the need for Japan to adapt to the normality of the twenty-first century – that of sharing global responsibility – rather than adopting the type of assertive great-power sovereignty typical of the nineteenth. Like Dr Vladimir Ivanov in his paper (presented by Pierre Lellouche), Inoguchi stressed that no durable move by Japan away from a policy of hedging its bets on the international scene was likely without domestic support. Inoguchi also stressed that although change in Japanese security policy was incremental, it could nonetheless be considerable over time.

The discussion initially focused on Japan's difficulty in reaching decisions and its reluctance to accept responsibility and take initiatives as a global actor, particularly on security issues. Some participants pleaded for caution when urging Japan to play a more vigorous global role, stressing the need to define very clearly what is envisaged. But the dominant current of opinion was quite critical of the slow rate at which Japan is becoming more active, and several speakers suggested that the conservatism of Japanese behaviour is counterproductive to Japanese interests because it is increasingly out of step with the pace of the world developments which affect those interests.

One example repeatedly cited was the low profile Japan has adopted during the General Agreement on Tariffs and Trade (GATT) talks, in whose outcome Japan has a very major stake. Another was the intransigence of Japanese policy on the territorial dispute with Russia. Several European participants suggested that such behaviour over a set of small islands contradicted the common interest, shared by Japan, in preventing disaster in Russia and preserving a moderate government there. Others demurred, arguing that it was presumptuous for outsiders to define Japanese interests, pointing out that it in fact had a smaller vested interest in the outcome in Russia than did Europe, and noting that preservation of the impasse bought Japan's leaders time by deferring the moment when a new rationale for the security relationship with the US would have to be articulated.

There was general agreement that much of the intractability in Japanese policy as a whole has been caused by the nature of the internal decision-making and leadership-selection processes, which encourage immobility and tend to penalize initiative and change. Some Japanese participants saw elements of hope in the emergence in recent years of younger Liberal Democratic Party leaders who have been pressing, thus far unsuccessfully, both for major structural reforms in the Japanese electoral and decision-making system, and for an invigoration of Japanese foreign policy to confront new international circumstances more directly.

Many participants saw the immobility of Japanese policy as closely connected with the refusal of the Japanese elite consensus to acknowledge the reality of Japanese behaviour during the Second World War. A lively, not to say abrasive, exchange took place on this score between a US and a Japanese participant.

Finally, there was a consensus that a central problem – and requirement – for the future is the preservation of the Japanese security tie to the United States. Indeed, the generally stabilizing role of continuous US engagement in the East Asian region has been a common thread of the proceedings. The main problem here is the possibility that Congressional budget pressures in America may eventually erode or even eliminate this military relationship. The key danger identified by some in the Committee is the possibility that under such extreme circumstances, new security dangers could impel Japan towards militarization and even the acquisition of nuclear weapons were the regional environment to evolve in a threatening fashion.

Committee 3

Dr Jonathan Pollack, in discussing 'The United States in East Asia: Holding the Ring', underscored the powerful reasons which continue to induce East Asia as a whole to seek cooperation with the US in the post-Cold War world. Overall, he drew the picture of a United States which would continue to play a key role in the region provided it still led the global trading system and maintained a military presence in East Asia. Pollack, as were others, was sceptical of European-style multilateral security arrangements in the Asian context: the bilateral tier would remain paramount.

His contention that the US would play the role of a balancing power in South-east Asia was not disputed; nor was there much argument against his analysis of the lack of applicability of the erstwhile 'US–USSR–China' triangle to future US–Chinese–Japanese relations, not least in view of Japan's quest for a 'normal' international role, rather than for a hegemonic regional position; hence a continued US–Japanese security alliance would remain desirable from Tokyo's perspective.

Differing views on the impact of the US presence on domestic developments and decision-making among Asian states were expressed. But there was broad agreement that American engagement and limited military presence was a stabilizing factor: in South-east Asia it provided insurance against China and Japan.

Similarly, in the case of North-east Asia, it was noted that if a US withdrawal occurred, other states in the region (e.g., Korea and China) would rightly or wrongly conclude that Japan would re-arm on a substantial scale. Regarding Korea, there was no visible disagreement with the proposition that a US presence would be of benefit during the reunification process.

One of the more interesting aspects of the Committee's proceedings was that while most Asians agree that a US military presence is a crucial factor sustaining strategic stability, Americans themselves tended to lack a clear understanding of their intrinsic interests in Asia and the Pacific. This naturally had an impact on the burden-sharing debate, even if America's military engagement in the Asia–Pacific region was a 'bargain, rather than a burden'. However, America could not provide regional stability on its own, which led the Committee to suggest ways of reducing America's burden. If what matters to the Asian countries is America's commitment and reliability (and not simply a force presence), then a large share of American engagement could be accomplished equally well by non-military means of engagement. Just as the US has sought 'places not bases' in South-east Asia, it may be that the US can, in a measured and deliberate way over time, follow this precedent in North-east Asia. For reasons of their own, the Americans may decide one day to disengage from the region, leaving East Asia to fend for itself. Perhaps the best safety net against resulting instability would be an incipient security dialogue, such as the ASEAN Post-Ministerial Conference (PMC), annual Asia–Pacific Economic Cooperative (APEC) summits and a forum for North-east Asian countries.

Committee 4
'Managing Korean Reunification' was examined from two different angles by Dr James Cotton and Professor Byung-joon Ahn. The former

made the point that current international (and notably US) pressure on North Korea may actually favour regime survival in Pyongyang; foreign pressure generates a combative response by the regime, thus making it politically easier for limited economic reform to slip in. Professor Ahn drew the Committee's attention to the possibility that Seoul may have to face a scenario rather different from the one it prefers of gradual, orderly and negotiated reunification-building on a succession of non-proliferation and arms-control measures, political *rapprochement* and a Yemeni-like agreement on reunification. Sudden reunification with tremendous costs could well occur – a point also underscored in Plenary IV by Dr Chung-min Lee and Professor Robert O'Neill. On this point, the Committee broadly concurred, pointing to the sudden collapse of the East German regime. The best policy for Seoul was to pursue incremental change while preparing for chaotic developments in a North devoid of a civil society: in effect, hoping for the best while preparing for the worst.

The North Korean nuclear option received a thorough airing. There was a consensus that the North Korean nuclear programme represented the greatest barrier to North–South reconciliation. Participants elaborated on some of the regional problems that would be created by North Korean acquisition of nuclear weapons, paying particular attention to its effect on the debate about militarization in Japan. Japanese participants stated that such an eventuality would not in itself cause Japan to pursue a nuclear option, but it would fuel spending on conventional forces in Japan.

Several participants observed that Pyongyang has played the nuclear card quite effectively in its dealings with the US and South Korea, although Kim Il-sung may be reaching the limit of what he can extract from it. On the question of the verification and monitoring of the North Korean nuclear programme, the Iraqi experience gives little reason for confidence, although challenge inspections would represent a major step forward and would satisfy politically the South Korean government. South Korean participants were urged to help the Committee understand the political, economic and social aspects of the North Korean situation. Most of the subsequent discussion was cautionary – stressing the uniqueness of the *juche* (self-reliance) experiment in the North and the fundamental differences between North and South. The paucity of reliable information about the Kim Il-sung regime encouraged all participants to look for instructive lessons from recent events, not least in Germany. Most of these lessons, however, fostered pessimism.

The Committee also turned its attention to the role of key international actors in the unification process, and notably to the issue of a regional equivalent of the 'Two Plus Four' formula. Much of the preliminary discussion (by non-Koreans) reflected a degree of interest in an institutionalized 'Two Plus Four' approach to unification. Korean participants took charge at this point and built an effective argument against such a formula since it is based upon an inappropriate analogy with the European case; it injects numerous external problems into North–South discussions and represents an unjustified imposition on Korean sovereignty. In the face of these arguments a consensus appeared to develop in support of a non-institutional *de facto* 'Two Plus Four' approach – the continued active involvement of China, the US, Japan and Russia in support of confidence-building and unification on the peninsula, but not a formal body.

The debate in Plenary IV came back to this issue: the point was made that 'catastrophic' reunification could well call for a 'One Plus Three' formula: the reuniting peninsula on the one hand, with Japan, the EC and the US handling international support on the other.

One point of disagreement among the Korean participants was of particular interest. This related to the legal status of North Koreans who move to South Korea. The general impression was that the South Korean case differs from the German case in that there is no automatic right of citizenship. The point is worth pursuing since it has obvious implications for the process of North–South union, particularly in view of the very large number of separated families.

Finally, there was a striking absence, what Sherlock Holmes called 'the dog that did not bark' – the total lack of discussion relating to the issue of US troops in South Korea.

Committee 5

In view of the broad agenda of Committee 5 on 'The Consequences of Nuclear and Conventional Arms Proliferation in Asia', a degree of division of labour was established beforehand between Dr Gerry Segal's broad-spectrum paper, Chancellor Ro-Myung Gong's focus on conventional arms and Ambassador Ryukichi Imai's concentration on nuclear issues.

Gerry Segal contrasted the sudden change in strategic fortunes, with post-Cold War Europe suddenly becoming the seat of conflict, whereas Asia had become much more peaceful than in previous decades while engaging in the most massive proliferation of weapons of mass destruction.

The dangers of conventional weapons proliferation were clearly underscored in Chancellor Gong's paper: in effect, a classical 'action–reaction' arms race spiral beginning to take hold in East Asia, which could, if left unchecked, lead to actual hostilities.

He suggested that a multilateral security dialogue needed to be developed in the Asia–Pacific region, along the broad lines recommended by Segal (albeit with variations on the kind of body which should be involved in the dialogue).

Ambassador Imai made a number of points which drew debate in the Committee, notably that if a nuclear threat were to emerge in Korea, Japan should consider an anti-tactical ballistic missile (ATBM) network, relying on early-warning and observation satellites using the (troubled) Japanese H-2 launcher. The Committee considered arms proliferation in Asia in two categories, potential and actual. The 'potential' category relates primarily to nuclear weapons. Here, there were a number of conflicting views. One was that it takes time to produce nuclear weapons and so we should not over-react to the North Korean threat. After all, the world has lived with six or seven nuclear states, so a few more would not matter. However, this view was not widely supported by the Committee and there was broad agreement that to do nothing would send out the wrong signals. The issue had to be tackled globally. More money had to be spent on the International Atomic Energy Agency (IAEA), and the global non-Proliferation regime should be strengthened. There might also be a role for Japan with investment in the global protection against limited strikes (GPALS) variant of the Strategic Defense Initiative (SDI) and the wider use of surveillance satellites.

Speakers from Russia and Kazakhstan refuted the argument that the collapse of the USSR had resulted in an increase in the contribution of the former Soviet Union to nuclear proliferation.

Little time was spent on missile or chemical and biological weapons proliferation, although it was suggested that South Korea, North Korea and Taiwan should join the Missile Technology Control Regime (MTCR).

There was no disagreement with the fact that Asian countries have been purchasing conventional arms at an increased rate, notably for power projection purposes, although it did not follow that these acquisitions were necessarily destabilizing. The ASEAN countries, South Korea, Taiwan and even to some extent China and India, have purchased arms as part of a general modernization process. Many are thus moving from land-oriented forces, concerned with internal security, to more balanced conventional forces.

However, these purchases generate genuine security fears. Unlike the binary situation in Cold War Europe, there are interlocking threat perceptions with areas of concern including the Chinese action in the South China Sea, the Korean peninsula, Taiwan's fear of China and a general concern about Japan: everybody mistrusts everybody else. In such a context a US withdrawal from the region was generally deemed to be destabilizing.

The Committee agreed that the potential for miscalculation needs to be reduced. There is thus the need for a mechanism to allay fears, and top-level political dialogues are necessary because the problems are more political than technical. A variety of expressions was used to characterize possible multilateral security mechanisms: 'à la carte', 'building blocks', 'transparency' – not to mention Yukio Satoh's 'multiplex' approach. Whereas nuclear proliferation required a global approach, conventional weapons proliferation pointed to the need for an Asian approach to developing mechanisms to promote stability.

Committee 6

Committee 6 on 'The Regional Impact of a Reforming India' addressed the question posed by Sir Michael Howard in Plenary I – would the subcontinent become prey to the centrifugal forces of ethnicity – an issue of some importance since it directly involves a fifth of the world's population. Professor Raju Thomas' point that internal violence was more of a security concern than external threat perception drew no challenge.

Dr Stephen Cohen's paper reaffirmed the absolute primacy of Pakistan's policies – and indeed existence – in determining Indian external security policy. This has not helped India recover its balance after being particularly affected by the end of the Cold War. Indeed, without a major strategic and defence debate, India may well miss the opportunity of playing a leadership role on the international scene: for as in the past, India wishes to be considered a leader, but is giving little thought to what this role implies – and in practice remains polarized on its immediate neighbourhood.

Indeed, from the Committee's proceedings it emerged that the likely immediate future of the subcontinent is Janus-faced: one face points to economic restructuring and liberalization; and the other points to increasing disarray and possible disintegration fuelled by ethnic, class and caste cleavages and secessionist schisms.

India's impact on the South Asian region (and by extension on the wider world of the Indian Ocean and the diaspora of Indians overseas) will vary considerably depending on which of these alternative futures predominates.

Unsurprisingly, it was agreed that India today is the dominant power in its region and will remain so unless it suffers dissolution of the Union because of communalism, mounting ethnic conflict and secessionism. Furthermore, Pakistan has a more fragile state structure and is more likely to disintegrate than India. It was argued, however, that throughout South Asia, the state has frittered away its claims to legitimacy and authority and often cannot really prove able to protect its citizens. The state is thus often seen as an oppressor not a protector.

Nonetheless the view was strongly and persuasively urged in the Committee that the present elite in the Indian government and armed forces share the common view, and value, that a united India will persist, and that all the secessionist tendencies can be contained, even if not resolved.

There was a wide-ranging discussion on the nuclear issue. It was noted that some 'hawkish' Indians argue for nuclear status as the only really convincing emblem and proof of great-power status. Consideration was given to the idea of offering India permanent membership of the UN Security Council as a means of bringing India within the Nuclear Non-Proliferation Treaty (NPT); however, no one thought it likely that a nuclear-free zone for South Asia would materialize in the near future.

The nature, pace and significance of India's present reform programme drew much discussion. The programme is far from clear-cut or from being smoothly implemented, and its chances of success remain problematic.

One possible wild card was mentioned in this respect: Indian geologists have said that there are tremendous and as yet mostly untapped oceanic oil resources within India's Exclusive Economic Zone.

There was discussion of the implications of the new constellation of Islamic forces to India's west and north, noting that this was a rather volatile constellation. Possibly more worryingly, Islamic fundamentalism inside India itself could have adverse repercussions, given a large Muslim population of approximately 110 million. These uncertainties are aggravated by the increasing assertion of a Hindu identity by a variety of mass parties, with knock-on effects for India's Muslim population.

A final impression of the Committee's proceedings is that the affairs of South Asia are to a considerable extent semi-detached from the outside world, including East Asia. South Asia is likely to remain somewhat autonomous, something of a *cul-de-sac* in the contemporary international system.

Committee 7

Loose talk about 'the triad' did not prevail in the hard-nosed approach Committee 7 took to 'What Role for Europe in Asian Affairs?', and there was little expectation of basic change in the relatively weak security and political links between western Europe and Asia. Indeed, François Godement subtitled his paper 'The Missing Link', and concluded without much opposition that 'any talk of a "triangle" can only be speculation'. He made the case that Asia's advantage in dealing with an open, single European market needed to be balanced by the opening of Asia to European hi-tech firms under conditions comparable to those given to US aerospace and electronic enterprises – a view which many in Europe would endorse. However, the quasi-absence of the Group of Seven (G-7) in Godement's analysis of future Euro-Asian relations was somewhat bemusing. Conversely, Fumiaki Takahashi emphasized the importance of the G-7 and other multilateral bodies as the means by which to manage the multipolar post-Cold War world. In the discussion, useful suggestions were made concerning the revamping of the G-7 machinery, which was currently oriented towards communiqué-drafting, rather than problem-solving, as demonstrated by the lack of action at the G-7 Summit in Munich last July on the burning issue of preventing a new Chernobyl in the former Soviet Union. The potential of the G-7 could be more fully exploited.

The Committee had to face some problems of definition: the notion of Europe and Asia (East Asia in this instance). If Europe reaches from Lisbon to Vladivostok, then it is a continent with a clear Pacific dimension; or should Europe be identified with the EC alone? What about the Asian policy of EC member-states, such as Great Britain (Hong Kong) or France (South Pacific)? Moreover, Europe and East Asia are different entities in structural and functional terms. Europe in its various definitions has a developed institutional framework of regional cooperation largely lacking in Asia.

The Committee attempted to define common interests (such as nuclear non-proliferation) or areas of friction (such as trade issues, arms sales, reconstruction of Russia and human rights). At the same time, it was pointed out that with the collapse of the Soviet Union one could no longer speak about a strong common security interest between Europe and Asia. If various areas of common interest and disagreement could thus be readily identified by the experts, they are not widely shared by politicians and public opinion in Europe and Asia. Indeed, there was hardly any suggestion of a really serious conflict between Europe and East Asia, be it in an economic or security field.

Multilateral frameworks of cooperation between Europe and Asia were examined, with emphasis being placed on the limits to multilateral fora for reasons dwelt upon in other Committees as well.

The problem of Russia's European and Asian nature was much discussed. Europeans emphasized that Japan and the rest of Asia share with them common interests in restructuring and developing Russia, but this view was not fully supported, not least by a Japanese delegate.

One Russian participant emphasized that there is a discrepancy in the security situation in Europe and Asia. In Europe there exists a developed framework of institutional cooperation with the Conference on Security and Cooperation in Europe (CSCE) or the North Atlantic Cooperation Council (NACC) which is lacking in Asia. This, in his view, helped explain why the reduction of Russian armed forces is more advanced in Europe than in Asia.

All in all, this Committee suffered from the scarcity of Asian participants, yet another manifestation of the weakness of Euro-Asian political and security relations. But as one participant put it: why should the Europeans be worried about the weakness of their security involvement in East Asia? After all, East Asia does not overly worry about its own lack of involvement in European security.

Plenary III
In examining the security relations between Russia and the other independent republics of the former USSR in Asia, Dr Sergei Karaganov described the wholly new and ambiguous situation which has emerged in the space of less than a year. A Russia which remains a great power in terms of territory and nuclear weapons, but which otherwise is a medium power, representing only about half of the former USSR's population. A Russia which has in effect little to fear from the South thanks to the appearance of Central Asian 'buffer

states', but also of a Russia which has increased its involvement in Central Asia in order to forestall the sort of destabilization which already affects the Caucasus and Tajikistan. A Russia which is politically as well as economically part of the Third World, and which may be tempted to search for Asian rather than Western alliances if the latter become synonymous with the failure of reform; but a Russia which is simultaneously impeded from finding an Asian location, in view of Japan's reticence and China's own ambition, and given its European demographic centre of gravity.

This drew a direct riposte from Dr John Chipman. A country which feels the need to identify with several geopolitical areas – such as France in the 1950s with 'Eurafrique', extending from Dunkirk to Tamanrasset – will tend to be a weak and uncertain power; 'Asians in Asia, Europeans in Europe, Democrats in the World', to use Minister Kozyrev's expression, may be a pleasing formula, but is it much more than that? Central Asia itself is heterogeneous; even Kazakhstan, which is in a category of its own, may well be inherently unstable given its '40–40–20' ethnic structure (which is not unlike that of Bosnia-Herzegovina), although this was questioned by some from the floor. And ambiguity marks Russia's relations with what are both independent states and members of the Commonwealth of Independent States (CIS), as it is still known – not unlike the role of France in post-colonial francophone Africa, but with fewer chances of success than France had: the internal situation of the new states, the regional context and Russia's financial weakness will see to that. There is great uncertainty over who makes Central Asian policy in Russia: is it the Ministry of Foreign Affairs, the armed forces, the intelligence services or a putative 'CIS Ministry'?

Chipman's bottom line was that Russia, and indeed the West (including Turkey), will only be accepted in the region if they are not seen to be immediately compromised by their association with the present generation of Central Asian leaders which may well be pushed out of power.

In the subsequent debate, the point was made that Russia could hardly take action in Central Asia on its own shoulders. There was also discussion of the effects of the possible disintegration of Russia: this could lead to Kazakhstan taking over the nuclear weapons on its territory; in the Russian Far East, such disintegration could hardly lead to economic opportunities for its Asian neighbours, since disintegration would most probably imply violence.

The ethnic repercussions of Central Asian independence on relations with China was mentioned, with opportunities for friction due notably to the numerous Kazakhs who live in Xinjiang, and the Uighurs residing in Kazakhstan.

Finally, the limits of models – Turkish, Malaysian, South Korean and so on – as a guide for policy was underlined.

Plenary IV

Dr Chung-min Lee, as one of South Korea's rising analysts, presented the picture of a strategic future not unlike that which is favoured by the Conference on Security and Cooperation in Asia (CSCA)-minded 'multilateralist' school. His conclusions can be summarized as follows:

- Although the United States' leverage will decline, the US will remain the only unifying actor in the region which should include the presence of a US force with clearly defined missions thus discouraging a regional arms race. But this may be more politically acceptable in Asia than in the US Congress; in his paper and in the debate, Lee also recommended giving greater attention to the budding trilateral defence dialogue between the US, Japan and South Korea.
- Security and defence policies in the region will be increasingly national, rather than collective; domestic factors will have crucial influence.
- A united Korea will be an important power in its own right, rather than an extension of great-power rivalry, even if unification may be a dramatic as well as a costly task. South Korea needs to prepare itself in the security arena as well as in domestic terms: it will need to reassess its relations with its neighbours.
- Creative muddling through with emphasis on domestic, national and bilateral aspects of security is the best hope, given the diversity of political, economic, strategic and territorial situations.

In his response, Robert O'Neill pleaded the cause of multilateralism with eloquence. Since the UN runs the risk of being overburdened, North-east Asia needs to generate a multilateral structure of its own, albeit one resembling ASEAN rather than the European model: socio-economic aspects of security rather than the politico-military ones. Such an organization would facilitate the interconnection and modernization of regional transportation and communications networks, together with access to Russian resources and developments such as the Tumen River project. Such a structure could also play a role in easing the strains of Korean reunification. As he put it in the debate, multilateralism had to build on a sense of both gain and pain, the gain of its presence (as in NATO Europe), the pain of its absence (as in the Korean War).

The subsequent debate dwelt substantially on China's role: will a bilaterally minded China move to a multilateral stance within the next five years, as Robert O'Neill suggested? How will domestic change affect the People's Republic of China's approach to the Taiwan issue? In order to pre-empt the regional consequences of friction concerning Taiwan, it was suggested that a maritime security zone be established in the seas bordering Korea, China and Japan, and notably in the straits of Tsushima.

Criticism was levelled at the inward-looking tendency of the North-east Asian area: it was argued that this could be alleviated by Korean reunification, and active participation in international development assistance and peacekeeping operations. Similarly criticism was directed at the insufficient place given to South-east Asia's role in East Asian affairs.

In his concluding remarks Dr Lee emphasized the crucial importance of Japan and Korea moving away from a zero-sum approach. Coming to terms with history, together with a close dialogue on political issues, could help achieve that aim, which could also build on the trilateral format involving the US.

Conclusion

It is apt that my last Annual Conference as Director of the IISS should have been held in Seoul, South Korea, on Asia's place in the world – for there is every sign that as one chapter of history closes, another opens in Europe as in Asia; when my first ex-officio Annual Conference, the Institute's 30th, was held in Brighton, it was clear that extraordinary events were in the offing which were to reshape radically Europe's strategic physiognomy and its place in the international system. Europe had the dubious privilege during the Cold War of being an exceptional continent: exceptional not only in its physical partition, but also in its strategic stability. That chapter has closed: now Europe has become an ordinary continent, beset by the same conflicts, the same effervescence, as others. In the case of Asia, a rather different type of chapter has closed: that of weak Asian influence on an international system structured by the Cold War and the existence of multiple conflicts often linked (as in Indochina and Afghanistan) to the broader setting imposed by the confrontation between the two superpower alliances. A new chapter is opening in Asia: the rise of a largely self-defined strategic system, which will in turn have a major impact on the new world order, or disorder. If East Asia is less directly affected than Europe by the end of the Cold War, the indirect effects will be considerable, as Asian countries grow in stature at the same time that the international system becomes largely unstructured.

I have had the great fortune of witnessing the demise of the Cold War order in Europe and the former Soviet Union; my successor will have the equally stimulating task of analysing, and drawing the implications of, a strategic revolution in which Asia's role will be of particular importance. As I hand over to Bo Huldt, I would wish to make three brief remarks.

First, our Institute has witnessed an exceptional period in its history, in which it had to shift the centre of gravity of its research effort previously anchored in the realities of the Cold War. We also had to adopt a *modus operandi* capable of analysing rapidly evolving situations, quite uncharacteristic of the East–West confrontation in Europe. When my predecessor, Robert O'Neill, summed up the proceedings of his last Annual Conference in Barcelona in 1986, he likened his experience at the IISS to a high-wire act, adding that he had enjoyed every minute of it. Well, so have I, but my own metaphor is that of a white-river rafter shooting a non-stop set of turbulent rapids – a thrilling sensation if not a restful one! It was thanks to the prior decisions of the Institute's governing bodies and successive Directors that this perilous passage occurred without the Institute losing its cohesion, integrity or sense of direction under the strain: an Institute in which regional conflict was already being analysed in its own right and in which the bulk of the Research Associates was changed every year had the sort of foundations which would allow it to withstand even paradigmatic earthquakes.

Second, the Institute's finances are in good order; the Institute's budget is in reasonable balance and the five-year capital appeal stands at around $3.3 million in hand raised in the midst of a global recession, one-third of the way to its target, with a completion date in late 1995. Furthermore, the current state of the London property market and our financial situation allow us to explore the prospect of moving to new quarters, either in a redeveloped Tavistock Street or in a new building, with improved research, library and meetings facilities. However, financial complacency is not in order: the capital appeal must now catch its second wind, notably in the USA. Furthermore, we must assume that for some years foundation grants will not be as plentiful for international affairs research as it has been: the inward-looking mood in the US is increasingly reflected in foundation funding. Hence the added urgency of an expanded capital base to fund an increased share of our research and to attract researchers on sabbatical.

Lastly, and most importantly, I would wish to thank you all, and through you, to thank our membership as a whole. I say this not *pro forma*, for the Institute ultimately rests on two pillars: the relevance and timeliness of its research on the one hand, which in turn rests on the creativity and motivation of our staff; the quality, expertise, geographical spread and loyalty of our members on the other. Indeed, at a time when the alliances of the Cold War are necessarily questioned, the fact that we have a particularly strong membership, in East Asia as well as in North America and Europe, is of more than passing significance, with robust national committees in Japan and in Korea (a Korean National Committee which I may say has done a terrific job to help make this conference a success): this membership base ensures that the IISS will continue to have the capability to bridge intellectually the gaps which the current strategic continental drifts tend to open between allies.

Council members, and members of the Institute, it has been a great privilege to work with you, and it has also been great fun: thank you for it all. As I move to the world of industry, investing some of my time in the nascent French committee of the IISS, I look forward to further Institute successes under Bo Huldt's stewardship.